RALPH C. LOSEY

e-Discovery for Everyone

Cover design by Cory Ottenwess / ABA Design

Printed in the United States of America.

20 19 18 17 16 5 4 3 2 1

ISBN: 978-1-63425-667-4
e-ISBN: 978-1-63425-668-1

Discounts are available for books ordered in bulk. Special consideration is given to state bars, CLE programs, and other bar-related organizations. Inquire at Book Publishing, ABA Publishing, American Bar Association, 321 N. Clark Street, Chicago, Illinois 60654-7598.

www.shopABA.org

Praise for *e-Discovery for Everyone*

"Attorneys can no longer claim to be confused by e-discovery! This book is a tremendous resource that makes e-discovery accessible for any legal professional, no matter past experiences with technology and the law–this is a "must-have" for any professional in the e-discovery industry, or trying to learn the industry."

Mark R. Williams–CEO and President of Kroll Ontrack, Inc.

"Losey is a master at making e-discovery accessible and even fun."

John Tredennick–Founder, CEO of Catalyst Repository Systems; past Chair of the ABA Law Practice Management Section

If there were an award in the legal profession for 'most creative iconoclast,' I'd be honored to present it to Ralph Losey for his short, entertaining, and provocative lessons in e-discovery. In 19 easy-to-read essays, Ralph adroitly weaves pop culture, science, technology, and astute case law analysis into the warp and weft of ethical responsibility and justice. All of us should wear the resulting cloth every day in our practice, if for no other reason than it itches, which is a good thing."

Kenneth J. Withers–Deputy Executive Director, The Sedona Conference®

"Ralph Losey is an acknowledged 'early starter' yet continuing thought leader in e-discovery and all the complexities that go into that phrase. Anything he does is well worth the read!"

Ronald J. Hedges, Senior Counsel for Dentons; former U.S. Magistrate Judge

"Ralph Losey has done it again: he is the Thomas Paine of e-discovery, with another excellent set of essays making the case that lawyers should follow 'commonsense' principles when dealing with the brave new world of electronically stored information. These principles include, first and foremost, litigators working as a team with e-discovery lawyers and outside specialists to ensure that discovery obligations are met. Second, they include lawyers recognizing that the newly amended Federal Rules of Civil Procedure emphasize that opposing counsel are expected to work cooperatively together to narrow areas of disagreement, and that lawyers should keep in mind that discovery should be proportional to the matters at stake in litigation. And third, lawyers should maintain competence on technical subjects, such as how to search through large volumes of digital data. This book is an easy (and fun to read) introduction to some of the most important topics in e-discovery. There is no better "explainer-in-chief" of e-discovery writing today!"

Jason R. Baron, Drinker Biddle & Reath LLP,; former Director of Litigation at the U.S. National Archives and Records Administration

"Litigation lawyers must envy estate lawyers. When was the last time the Rule Against Perpetuities changed? These days, since all discovery and litigation is electronic discovery and litigation, the poor litigator has to absorb technological and rule changes, new cases, and the very definition of their competence and ethical obligations. It is a good thing they have Ralph Losey and this collection of essays. Ralph is utterly fearless and, unlike many of his colleagues, welcomes technological changes and insists that their often drastic implications for the courts, lawyers, and society be considered soberly and realistically. He is as comfortable with the insights of social psychology, philosophy, and mathematical reasoning as he is with metadata. And the man refuses to be dull. His book is full of song lyrics, truly corny jokes, and clever drawings. Over the years, Ralph has forced us to look beyond our narrow concerns and try to see where all this change is taking us. This is a most welcome book."

John M. Facciola, U.S. Magistrate Judge for the U.S. District Court for the District of Columbia (retired); Adjunct Professor of Law, Georgetown Law School

Contents

I dedicate this book to my wife, Molly,
who has been my safe harbor in all storms.

About the Author

Ralph C. Losey is a principal of Jackson Lewis, P.C., a labor and employment law firm in the United States with more than 800 attorneys. He is the firm's *National e-Discovery Counsel* in charge of electronic discovery services and training. Mr. Losey also heads the firm's litigation support department, which, under his leadership, the firm outsourced to a major vendor. Mr. Losey personally performs the predictive coding work in multiple document review projects each year and supervises and consults in many others, including the *Da Silva Moore* case, where predictive coding was first approved by a court. Mr. Losey has also won a document review contest supervised by a major university and nonprofit group. He classified 1.7 million documents by himself in 64.5 hours, attaining the highest F1 scores among 19 contestants in both relevance and privilege search. In 2015 and 2016 Mr. Losey led a research team at the National Institute of Standards and Technology Text Retrieval Conference (TREC), where he participated in the total recall track to demonstrate his hybrid multimodal method of predictive coding. His published reports at TREC 2015 and 2016 can be found at one of Mr. Losey's educational websites, www.MrEDR.com.

Mr. Losey has specialized in electronic evidence and discovery since 2006, at which time he started and ran the e-discovery department at Akerman, LLP. In 2010, he joined Jackson Lewis. Prior to 2006, Mr. Losey handled a variety of commercial litigation, insurance, and technology cases, including one of the largest Qui Tam cases in history.

Mr. Losey has been a computer hobbyist since 1978 and an ethical hacker since the 1980s, at which time he created several original game and music software programs for his children. He also established and operated his law firm's information technology department from the early 1980s to early 1990s. In 2015, Mr. Losey was a finalist for the Legaltech CIO of the Year Innovation Award.

Mr. Losey has written more than 2 million words on law and technology subjects since 2006, including more than 60 articles on predictive coding. In 2006, he started his well-known blog, *e-DiscoveryTeam.com*, which later grew to include over a dozen legal education websites. His writings include seven books on e-discovery and technology published by the American Bar Association (ABA), McMillian, and West-Thompson, including a new book by the ABA to be released in 2016, where he serves as co-editor and contributor, *Perspectives on Predictive Coding.* He has also published four law review articles: *Predictive Coding and the Proportionality Doctrine*, 26 REGENT U. L. REV. 1 (2013–2014); *HASH: The New Bates Stamp*, 12 JOURNAL OF TECHNOLOGY LAW & POLICY 1 (June 2007); *Mancia v. Mayflower Begins a Pilgrimage to the New World of Cooperation*, 10 SEDONA CONF. J. 377 (2009 Supp.); and *Lawyers Behaving Badly*, 60 MERCER L. REV. 983 (Spring 2009).

Mr. Losey served as an adjunct professor at the University of Florida School of Law from 2007 to 2011, where he taught both introductory and advanced e-discovery courses. He developed the law school's first online course, which he later spun-off into a private instructional program, e-DiscoveryTeamTraining.com. Mr. Losey has lectured at many continuing legal education events and conferences around the world since 2006, with a focus over the last several years on predictive coding and overall best practices.

Mr. Losey received his B.A. from Vanderbilt University in 1973 and his J.D. with Honors from the University of Florida School of Law in 1979.

Foreword

Judge Paul Grimm
District Judge for the U.S. District Court for the District of Maryland

In the short span of a decade and a half, the practice of discovery of writings, recordings, photographs, and other nontestimonial evidence in civil cases in state and federal courts has transformed from one that was based almost entirely on the manual retrieval, review, and production of tangible documents by lawyers and paralegals to one that is almost entirely dependent on accessing, searching, reviewing, and producing digital—or computer-generated—information. The "digital explosion" has required fundamental revisions to the Federal Rules of Civil Procedure, first in 2006 and most recently in 2015, and even more fundamental changes in how lawyers and judges must think about discovery in civil cases. Along the way, many participants in the process of civil litigation felt as though they were called on to engage in a battle of wits for which they were unarmed—lacking the technical know-how to survive. While the newest members of the legal profession typically have greater knowledge (and less fear) regarding what is needed to engage in what has come to be known as "e-discovery," there are many lawyers and judges of a certain age who do not and who look at the process with concern—if not fear and loathing.

Part of the problem lies with not knowing where to begin to develop the knowledge and experience needed to survive in the daunting new world of e-discovery. To borrow a phrase famously used by a former Secretary of Defense, we "do not know what we don't know." Where do you turn to learn what the issues are, let alone how to resolve them? Most lawyers are not computer scientists, statisticians, or semanticists, and getting the training to be competent in using computer-assisted review (also called technology-assisted review [TAR]) to more effectively and inexpensively search large digital information sets seems beyond our grasp.

Enter Ralph Losey and the ABA with *e-Discovery for Everyone*, an introduction to e-discovery that avoids overtechnicality without being substantively superficial, while managing to be interesting and at times even amusing. Ralph has been writing his e-Discovery Team blog since 2006, and *e-Discovery for Everyone* assembles many of his most helpful blog posts in a collection that will be of value to newcomers to e-discovery as well as seasoned practitioners. The book is written in a conversational style and is divided into short chapters, which can be easily read in a relatively short sitting. Sprinkled throughout are very helpful references to cases, secondary sources, and other materials that give the book depth beyond its relative brevity. A quick look at the table of contents shows an impressive inventory of the most important e-discovery topics of the day: new methods of search and review, a discussion of the 2015 amendments to the Federal Rules of Civil Procedure, practical advice on litigation holds, how to evaluate the reasonableness of e-discovery vendor bills, the advantages of transparency in selecting how to design a search for digital information, why cooperation during the e-discovery process is essential to success, ethical issues associated with e-discovery, and how to confront and control e-discovery abuses.

e-Discovery for Everyone provides a welcome addition to the literature on e-discovery. Like a well-designed website, it is easy to navigate, informative, interesting, comprehensive without being overwhelming, and enjoyable.

Introduction

A TEAM APPROACH TO E-DISCOVERY

Electronic discovery is a new area of the law that some lawyers think is hopelessly arcane and obtuse, or even boring. This book aims to prove them wrong by providing a friendly and interesting introduction to e-discovery. Although this is a fast-evolving specialty known for complex legal and technical issues, it is still possible to make an accessible introduction. The e-discovery niche has a few very dark corners, but we will shy away from the more advanced topics.

This book—my fifth on the subject—is not intended to be an all-inclusive textbook, but rather a friendly, intellectually stimulating introduction. It is composed of a series of stand-alone chapters derived from the most accessible posts in my law blog, e-DiscoveryTeam.com. It begins with general introductory chapters giving a broad, upbeat overview. The book then goes into my favorite e-discovery topic, legal search, with several chapters pertaining to the ins and outs of finding relevant evidence. That is the heart of all e-discovery. A key chapter comes after that, Chapter 6, on the 2015 amendments to the Federal Rules of Procedure: *The 2015 e-Discovery FRCP Rule Amendments and a Goldilocks Era of Proportional Discovery.* Next, I address a variety of interesting issues and difficulties that all litigators face in dealing with electronic discovery. The book concludes with a series of chapters on ethics. e-Discovery, more than any other field of law, is filled with ethical landmines. These chapters will help you to stay on the straight and narrow path and provide suggestions on how to deal with other counsel who do not.

Some attorneys try to avoid e-discovery entirely for fear of getting in over their heads and making horrible mistakes. Although there is some validity to this concern, it is overrated. There are both deep and shallow waters in this new field. Many areas of e-discovery legal practice are shallow, not deep, and they are not too difficult to learn. At this point in the stage of this field of law, most issues do not involve completely novel issues or complex data analytics, statistics, and arcane technologies. Instead, most e-discovery issues today can be solved using traditional legal reasoning. Common sense and good ethics will keep you out of the sanctions landmines that we often hear about in e-discovery.

My career path led me to becoming a full-time specialist in electronic discovery back in 2006. In 2010, I became the national e-discovery counsel for my firm Jackson Lewis, a labor and employment law firm with more than 800 attorneys, most of whom are litigators. In my role, I work daily with trial attorneys all over the country and have developed multiple e-discovery training programs. Most of the attorneys in our training programs have very little prior familiarity with e-discovery or computer systems. I know from experience that they can quickly learn how to handle most of the issues that arise. After some initial training, I still get calls from them, which is what I want, but they are typically only six-minute time entries. If the attorney or paralegal calling me has completed the firm's e-discovery training, they usually already know the answer. They call at first just to be sure that the answers they came up with are correct. Most of the time they are. Even with no prior experience or training, it is not hard to use traditional legal reasoning to come to the correct answers, especially if lawyers use the team approach that I advocate in my *e-Discovery Team* blog.

Most of e-discovery can be learned fairly quickly; however, like anything worthwhile, it requires hard work and persistent efforts. It is all challenging and fascinating, to be sure—especially if you enjoy technology—but deep computer expertise is *not* required for most of the problems. Most litigators find that they can work through the common issues seen in this field, if they learn to use a *team approach* to legal practice. This is an approach to legal practice where you routinely work with experts from outside of the law. e-Discovery requires working with nonlawyer experts in computer systems, forensics, data storage (in the clouds or in the office), data analysis, statistics, many kinds of software, and social media environments of all kinds.

The interdisciplinary team approach is a new skill for many lawyers, but it is one that must be learned to perform e-discovery properly. It is essentially a communication challenge. Think of Abbot and Costello's famous "Who's on First?" This is a work challenge, to be sure, but it is a manageable one. This kind of communication challenge is within the ability of all good litigators. As a group, we are all pretty good at the communication of complex issues. The primary obstacle for many lawyers in dealing with technology is the reluctance to admit inadequate knowledge and trying to go it alone. The "fake it until you make it" approach does not work here; you need to rely on others to help you to do it right. They can be experts employed by e-discovery vendors, other consultants, or specialists like myself. The team approach makes it easy to learn what you need to know in a particular case to properly represent your client.

This book will cover most e-discovery issues where the waters are not deep. A trusted e-discovery vendor can often provide the team you need to understand the technical issues. In a rare case where you must sail into deep waters and hazardous storms, then you can always enlist other team players to help. You may even have to bring in another lawyer who specializes in e-discovery. Complex, technical topics such as predictive coding and international data import issues come to mind.

Although e-discovery has its deep waters—places where math and statistics reign—it is overall just a new type of document production. It is discovery, which is something that all litigation attorneys and paralegals must learn to do. We cannot only do paper discovery. We have no choice but to also discover computer-generated information because nearly all information today is electronic. The evidence is in vast clouds of data; paper is just an incidental printout. All litigators today must be able to find this electronic evidence and perform e-discovery, but they do not have to do it alone.

An interdisciplinary team approach comes in here. In well-functioning teams, the lawyers are in charge, but other professionals play a significant role, including vendors and the occasional outside legal specialist. After years of working in this field, I am more convinced than ever that the best solution for most lawyers to the problem of e-discovery is to work with a team. Even if you only spend a couple of hours on e-discovery issues each month, you can still do an excellent job by using the team approach. You do not have to specialize, as I have done, but you do need the help and support of a team with technical skills and knowledge that you probably do not have.

Most attorneys need technology specialist team members to help them, typically engineers, not lawyers. Sometimes in very large-volume data cases, you may even need the help of data scientists who specialize in text retrieval. In every e-discovery team, a common language is the key to clear communication. The engineers and scientists have to understand the legal language, and vice versa.

Just like a sports team, a positive team spirit is also critical. Successful teamwork is always built on mutual respect, leadership, and goodwill. All team members must have a clear understanding of their role and the positions they play. Simply hiring the lowest-priced e-discovery vendor can be a recipe for disaster. It is also a big mistake (not to mention unethical) to simply turn everything over to a vendor to do it for you. You need a good working relationship with a vendor, but you do the law yourself. As mentioned, in rare circumstances, you may need help with the law too, in which case you should turn to legal specialists.

In some large law firms, all of the e-discovery team members are full-time firm employees, both lawyers and engineers. This is not necessary and can even be a mistake. Most lawyers and law firms, including my own, depend on e-discovery vendors to supply most of the nonlawyer members of their team. The law firm gives legal advice and leads the team, but relies on an outside company to provide the non-legal services. The team members outside of the law firm do not provide legal advice, but rather provide engineering advice and services. These team members work for e-discovery vendors outside of the law firm.

e-Discovery vendors cannot give legal advice; only law firms or attorneys in legal practice can do that. However, they can help in all other aspects of e-discovery, especially the very technical computer aspects. Law firms, even the largest, may also need to consult with various types of e-discovery specialist attorneys from time to time, but only for the most challenging tasks. Even specialists like myself need to consult with other specialists from time to time. For instance, I will not touch cross-border, international e-discovery issues. Conversely, because my e-discovery subspecialty is legal search and active machine learning, other specialists in the field ask me for help on that area from time to time.

e-Discovery is like a vast body of water. Most of it is shallow, as noted, and you should not fear to tread, but it does have a few deep, shark-infested areas. Stay alert and be ready to call in the Marines. Most e-discovery specialists are quite adept at helicoptering in and out of litigation war zones.

The key to all well-functioning professional teams is training and practice. e-Discovery team members, lawyers, paralegals, scientists, technicians, managers, and others must all learn a core body of knowledge on this new area of law and information technology. Competence is the key and competence comes through education and practice.[1] More information on this is provided in the concluding chapters of this book on ethics.

Education can take many forms, including books like this one, organized training by in-person programs (which I do a lot of for my law firm and its clients), and online training programs (see, for instance, the one I designed: e-DiscoveryTeamTraining.com). You can also avail yourself of traditional continuing legal education. Many education programs are very good, but do not expect too much from just listening to lectures or watching mock procedures. It takes time and effort to learn any legal field, including e-discovery, but I think you will find it is well worth it.

---

[1]*See ABA Model Rule 1.1 Comment 8* ("To maintain the requisite knowledge and skill, a lawyer should keep abreast of changes in the law and its practice, including the benefits and risks associated with relevant technology").

Computers are here to stay, and so too are lawyers that need to find the evidence necessary to defend or prosecute their cases. More and more, critical evidence will be found in computers and other electronic storage devices, both in offices, homes, the cloud, pockets, even on wrists. In the not-too-distant future, we may live in a world filled with artificial intelligence and an Internet cluttered with smart things. The data will literally be everywhere, from body implants to your refrigerator. This book, and a good team, will help prepare you to meet the future with confidence—and hopefully, a bit and byte of good humor.

1 We Are at the Dawn of a Golden Age of Justice

The information explosion we are seeing now will inevitably trigger a justice explosion when law catches up with technology. It will happen as soon as law learns to harvest the key evidence needed to resolve lawsuits from the vast new mountains of digital information that technology is creating. When that happens, we will enjoy a much higher level of justice than we do now. More often, our judges and juries will reach better, more just decisions because they will know more of the truth. All justice is dependent on truth and objective facts. The technology revolution has created far more information than ever before. As the law learns to retrieve this information, there also will be far more justice than ever before.

In law, we find justice by the light of truth. We find truth by evidence of objective facts of past and present events and mental states. We find this truth through writings, the testimony of witnesses, and sometimes physical evidence, such as guns or fingerprints. Testimony is the oral account of witnesses as to the facts—what they saw, heard, and did. Although testimony is based upon solemn oaths to tell the truth, all lawyers and judges know that it is inherently subjective and never completely reliable. Testimony is built on the frailties of memory and observation. The great advances in technology have done little, if anything, to improve the reliability of our memory or our testimony. Our memory of facts remains as vague and subjective as ever. (Someday, the polygraph may reveal intentional lies but we are not there yet, and it will likely never reveal unintentional errors or subjective coloring.)

The law has learned that testimony only leads to a reasonably accurate account of objective facts when supplemented with writings (and physical objects, when applicable) made at the time of the events in question. Writings (traditionally called *documents* in the law) are understood in the broadest sense to include not only paper (the mere tip of the iceberg) but all electronic information, including videos and computer records. Writings are the guardians of truth—the refreshers of memory that keep people honest. They are the best, most accurate repository of objective facts and have been for centuries.

This should give us great hope for the future of justice because the extent and complexity of writings are now exploding exponentially. As soon as lawyers learn to search and retrieve this new explosion of electronic evidence, cases will be decided on more and better documentary evidence than ever before. Testimony will become more reliable because it will be checked and constrained by more contemporaneous writings. A new dawn of justice will become possible as intentional and unintentional lies are exposed. We will be able to decide cases based on more of the truth than ever before. The flood of new information and new writings will generate a new age of justice that far exceeds anything we have seen to date.

It is a good time to be a lawyer. If you can understand the tidal wave of new technologies and new writings, you can advance the cause of justice. You can find the writings needed for judges and juries to make their decisions based upon accurate evidence. The truth is out there in vastly greater quantities than ever before. Yes, it is intangible—just electronic pulses representing zeros and ones. Yes, it is sometimes hidden like a needle in a haystack. However, the truth can be found. It will be found by the lawyers of today and tomorrow as we learn e-discovery.

We can all tap into the information age to fill courts with truth. The days of justice based on paper and candlepower are over. Lawyers should instead sing the body electric.

2

e-Discovery Team Commandos: The e-Discovery Side of the Story of the Bin Laden Raid

One of the most dramatic events in recent history, the Osama Bin Laden raid, shows the importance of electronic discovery in all aspects of modern life, including the military. On May 2, 2011, U.S. Navy Seals carried out the most dramatic seizure of electronically stored information (ESI) in history. The ESI collection team also imposed immediate terminating sanctions on one of the most notorious ESI custodians in history.

The size and speed of the Seals' forensic collection of Bin Laden's ESI was impressive and near flawless. It was carried out by the legendary Seal Team Six—a senior, very elite group in the Seals who are specially trained in the detection and seizure of information. There is no better, nor more dangerous, e-discovery collection team in the world.

According to news reports, Seal Team Six helicoptered in and collected 10 hard drives, 10 cell phones, 5 to 10 computers, at least 100 computer disks (including thumb drives and DVDs), handwritten notes, documents, weapons, and an assortment of personal items. In all, 2.7 terabytes of data were collected. The team completed the whole project in just 38 minutes. They lost one helicopter in the process; however, as Judge Scheindlin said in the landmark *Pension Committee* case, no e-discovery project is perfect.[1]

The U.S. government immediately began sifting through these data at a secret site in Afghanistan. An online news publication, *Politico*, claimed that an anonymous government source told them shortly after the raid that “hundreds of people are going through it now. It’s going to be great even if only 10 percent of it is actionable. They cleaned it out. Can you imagine what’s on Osama bin Laden’s hard drive?” It was “the motherlode of intelligence.”[2]

The Seals did not helicopter out with Bin Laden’s paper filing cabinet. They took his computers, his hard drives, his DVDs, and his thumb drives. They also took his life and his body. It was a good day for the United States. It was a good day for e-discovery.

The U.S. Office of the Director of National Intelligence has declassified and published some of the recovered ESI. The material can be found online.[3] Many of the documents are in English, including 30 software and technical manuals.

---

[1]The Pension Committee of the University of Montreal Pension Plan v. Banc of America Securities, LLC, 685 F. Supp. 2d 456, 456 (S.D.N.Y. 2010) (“In an era where vast amounts of electronic information is available for review, discovery in certain cases has become increasingly complex and expensive. Courts cannot and do not expect that any party can meet a standard of perfection.”)

[2]Politico, found at *http://www.politico.com/story/2011/05/exclusive-raid-yields-trove-of-data-054151,* accessed May 2, 2011.

[3]*See https://www.odni.gov/index.php/resources/bin-laden-bookshelf.*

Perspective on Legal Search and Document Review

3

For millennia, writings were on paper. For centuries, the legal profession depended upon writings (referred to in the law as *documents*) as the key evidence to resolve disputes in a fair and just manner.[1] Paper documents were well known and mastered by every lawyer and judge who swore an oath to uphold the law. This all changed in a historical blink of the eye. In just one generation, documents have dematerialized and transformed into a dizzying array of digital media.

NEW AGE OF TECHNOLOGY

Many see this new age of technology as a much more profound cultural revolution than that precipitated by Gutenberg, which took centuries to play out, not decades. Paul and Baron's well-known article explains how writing co-evolved with civilization over the past 50 centuries or longer, with a slow but steady increase in information as our writing technologies slowly improved.[2] As they

---

[1] Ralph Losey, *Mathematical Formula for Justice Proves the Importance of ESI in Civil Litigation*, in ELECTRONIC DISCOVERY (West 2010).

[2] George L. Paul & Jason R. Baron, *Information Inflation: Can the Legal System Adapt?* 13 RICH. J.L. & TECH. 10 (2007).

pointed out, the situation changed about 25 years ago when a totally different form of electronic writing was invented, free from physical confines, which triggered the explosion of a new universe of virtually unlimited information. Paul and Baron predicted that the legal profession would necessarily have to change significantly and adopt new strategies of practice to cope with this information revolution.

Documents originally created on paper still exist in our society, but they are rare.[3] Most of the paper documents we see are merely printouts of one dimension (the text) of the original electronic information. The law recognizes this transformation and the Federal Rules of Civil Procedure were amended in 2006 to include electronically stored information (ESI) as information that can be discovered and used as evidence in lawsuits.[4] ESI is not specifically defined in the rules. The Rules Committee commentary explained why:

> The wide variety of computer systems currently in use, and the rapidity of technological change, counsel against a limiting or precise definition of electronically stored information. Rule 34(a)(1) is expansive and includes any type of information that is stored electronically.[5]

Even without specific amendments to rules, all state and federal courts already treated ESI as potentially admissible evidence subject to discovery by 2006. The first Sedona Principle is now commonplace:[6]

> Electronically stored information is potentially discoverable under Fed. R. Civ. P. 34 or its state equivalents. Organizations must properly preserve electronically stored information that can reasonably be anticipated to be relevant to litigation.

---

[3]Zubulake v. UBS Warburg LLC, 217 F.R.D. 309, (S.D.N.Y. 2003). (FN 5 cites Wendy R. Liebowitz, *Digital Discovery Starts to Work*, NAT'L L.J., Nov. 4, 2002, at 4, reporting that 93 percent of all information generated in 1999 was already in digital form. I believe it is over 99 percent today.)
[4]Rule 34(a)(1), Federal Rules of Civil Procedure (2006).
[5]Rules Committee Commentary to the 2006 Amendments to Rule 34, Subdivision (a).
[6]*The Sedona Principles: Best Practices Recommendations & Principles for Addressing Electronic Document Production*, 2d (June 2007), available at *http://www.thesedonaconference.org*.

STRESSED-OUT LAWYERS

The legal profession has been severely stressed by the rapid, ever-accelerating advances in technology. The changes in writing and resulting information explosion have been the key stressors. ESI is not only changing and evolving into new forms every year, but it is now multiplying at an exponential rate that is almost beyond comprehension.[7] Most lawyers are unfamiliar with ESI and the complex systems that store it. They prefer the familiar paper and alphabetical filing cabinets. They are paper lawyers living in a digital world.

The astronomical volume and complexity of ESI has made the traditional process of legal discovery very expensive and burdensome. Many have called this a *crisis* in our legal system that threatens our system of justice.[8] The old methods to review digital writings that lawyers used for paper are too expensive. No one can afford the time and effort required to locate, review, and produce all relevant evidence using those old methods; the costs and burdens often exceed the value of the entire case. There is a real danger that the resolution of disputes in a court of law based on both testimony *and writings* will be a luxury available only to the wealthiest parties:

> [The articles in this Supplement] suggest that if participants in the legal system act cooperatively in the fact-finding process,

---

[7] *See, e.g.,* Rowe Entm't, Inc. v. William Morris Agency, Inc., 205 F.R.D. 421, 429 (S.D.N.Y. 2002) (explaining that electronic data is so voluminous because, unlike paper documents, "the costs of storage are virtually nil. Information is retained not because it is expected to be used, but because there is no compelling reason to discard it"), *aff'd*, 2002 WL 975713 (S.D.N.Y. May 9, 2002); *Data, Data Everywhere,* THE ECONOMIST (March 2010); Jason Baron & Ralph Losey, *E-Discovery: Did You Know?* video at *https://www.youtube.com/watch?v=bWbJWcsPp1M&list=FLiiloqmOaKR28OqcBJaEQrQ.*

[8] *Final Report on the Joint Project of the American College of Trial Lawyers and the Institute for the Advancement of the American Legal System* (2009) at 15 ("Although electronic discovery is becoming extraordinarily important in civil litigation, it is proving to be enormously expensive and burdensome."). More information is available at: *www.uscourts.gov/file/document/actl-iaals-report-2010-civil-litigation-conference.*

> more cases will be able to be resolved on their merits more efficiently, and this will help ensure that the courts are not open only to the wealthy. I believe this to be a laudable goal, and hope that readers of this Journal will consider the articles carefully in connection with their efforts to try cases.[9]

Even though many scholars, jurists, and practitioners recognize the problems created by the inability of lawyers to keep pace with technology, most law schools still only train students in paper evidence and discovery. Students graduate unprepared to handle ESI, where the truth of past events is now stored.[10] The law remains as dependent as ever on documents to prove the truth, but the vast majority of lawyers are untrained and unprepared to handle the electronic documents upon which the world is now built.[11] In fact, most lawyers—even those who specialize in litigation—dislike e-discovery and try their best to avoid it. Lawyers are trained and prepared instead to handle paper documents following systems developed in the 20th century.

OLD 20TH-CENTURY METHODS

Paper-based legal search and review methods are one dimensional and linear in nature. They typically follow a sequential Bates stamp organizational model created in the 1890s. The simple paper evidence discovery processes worked pretty well for decades before

---

[9] *See, e.g.,* Justice Stephen Breyer, *Preface*, SEDONA CONFERENCE J. 10 (Suppl., Fall 2009).

[10] William Hamilton, *The E-Discovery Crisis: An Immediate Challenge to our Nation's Law Schools*, ELECTRONIC DISCOVERY (West 2010); Shannon Capone Kirk & Kristin G. Ali, *Teach Your Children Well: A Case for Teaching E-Discovery in Law Schools*, Chapter 38 of ELECTRONIC DISCOVERY (West 2010); Shira Scheindlin & Ralph Losey, *E-Discovery and Education*, Chapter 33 of ELECTRONIC DISCOVERY (West 2010); Ralph Losey, *Plato's Cave: Why Most Lawyers Love Paper and Hate e-Discovery and What This Means to the Future of Legal Education*, Chapter 32 of ELECTRONIC DISCOVERY (West 2010).

[11] Ralph Losey, *E-Discovery Competence Is a Fundamental Ethical Challenge Now Faced by the Legal Profession*, ELECTRONIC DISCOVERY (West 2010).

computers. However, even before technology moved away from paper typing machines to computers in the 1980s, the discovery processes were already severely taxed by the growing volumes of paper documents generated from the 1960s onward. The increase in paper volume was caused by another technological innovation, the photocopy machine, and by increasingly complex transactions. Still, the legal profession coped for the rest of the 20th century. Lawyers added more numbers to the Bates stamps and used larger teams of lawyers and paralegals to manage the additional papers. They were still on familiar ground.

The linear systems developed in the 19th and 20th centuries for the discovery and production of documents, continue to be used today by most attorneys for both ESI and paper discovery.[12] This use of old paper-based systems with today's ESI is a big mistake and is the primary reason why e-discovery is so expensive.

PAPER-DERIVED PROCESSES AND METHODS FOR SEARCH AND REVIEW DO NOT WORK WHEN APPLIED TO HIGH VOLUMES OF ESI

Old linear review methods involved serial culling of documents down to a final production set. The process generally required multiple reviews of the same document for different purposes. It was inefficient and expensive. Moreover, the quality control of human eyes on paper did not work with high volumes of documents. This is shown by the scientific experiments where the agreement rate among professional legal reviewers was found to be just less than 50 percent.[13]

---

[12] *See, e.g.*, the *D'Onofrio* saga of four opinions by Judge Facciola, which describes the processes used in this case and his many orders resolving disputes, including an order requiring production of a sample of the 9,413 documents listed on the privilege log: D'Onofrio v. SFX Sports Group, Inc. 247 F.R.D. 43 (D.D.C. 2008); D'Onofrio v. SFX Sports Group, Inc. 254 F.R.D. 129 (D.D.C. 2008). The cases are described in Chapter 27 of my book ELECTRONIC DISCOVERY (West 2010).

[13] Gordon V. Cormack, Maura R. Grossman, Bruce Hedin & Douglas W. Oard, *Overview of the TREC 2010 Legal Track*, available at *http://trec.nist.gov/pubs/trec19/papers/LEGAL10.OVERVIEW.pdf* (accessed February 21, 2012).

This tradition of multiple manual reviews, with only limited computer assistance and typically on a linear-based review platform, still continues today. However, it is too expensive and inefficient with high volumes of ESI. This will only get worse as the amount of information continues to grow exponentially. Jason Baron, the former head of litigation for the National Archives and Records Administration (which is in charge of all federal records, including White House e-mail), explained this as a problem of scale. He projected that the number of White House e-mails will soon exceed 1 billion per decade. He estimates that it would cost more than $2 billion to search that many e-mails, which assumes a team of 100 full-time lawyers working over 54 years and a very low billing rate of $100 per hour. It also assumes computer-assisted review tools, but following the old paper-based linear review models.[14]

Moreover, too many mistakes are being made when these traditional linear review methods are applied to the astronomical volumes and new media of ESI:

> Plaintiff's counsel conceded at the hearing that the task of searching Plaintiff's records for relevant emails in response to Defendants' discovery request was entrusted to a junior associate. It is apparent that the associate worked with little or no direction or supervision. The search terms used by the associate were inadequate—they did not even include the term "phone"—and, as a result, she failed to locate or perceive the significance of the emails about which Defendants now complain.[15]

---

[14] Jason Baron, *Information Inflation: Can the Legal System Adapt?* at 13–15. *Also see* Jason Baron, *E-discovery and the Problem of Asymmetric Knowledge* (presented at the Mercer Law School Ethics in the Digital Age Symposium, Nov. 2008); *supra* note 2, at 5.

[15] Diabetes Centers of America, Inc. v. Healthpia America, Inc., 2008 U.S. Dist. LEXIS 8362, 2008 WL 336382 (S.D. Tex. Feb. 5, 2008). *Also see* Danis v. USN Communications, Inc., 2000 WL 1694325 (N.D. Ill. 2000) ($10,000 fine imposed against the chief executive officer personally when the young general counsel he hired to supervise ESI preservation was grossly negligent); Mt. Hawley Ins. Co. v. Felman Production, Inc., 2010 WL 1990555 (S.D. W. Va. May 18, 2010) (a serious mistake was made resulting in waiver of privilege despite sophisticated counsel with very elaborate processes and safeguards).

OUTSOURCING ALONE IS NOT THE ANSWER

Some are looking for an answer to these expense issues by keeping the old processes, but outsourcing the work of manual review to less expensive *contract* lawyers. They are called "contract lawyers" because the law firm that represents the client does not employ them. Instead, they work for the firm or some other company under a contract to do only review work. These contract lawyers may be located in India or other countries, down the street from your office, or down the hall.

Even if you accept the abilities of contract lawyers to adequately perform the task of the first-level relevance review (which I do, with qualifications), this is still just a stopgap measure. The volume of ESI is increasing exponentially. Outsourcing may help with expenses to a point, but it is still futile as a stand-alone long-term strategy; it is still just treading water in the midst of a flood. Indeed, when this outsourcing strategy was employed by the U.S. Department of Justice to try to reduce the costs of a privilege review, it still cost $9.09 per file to do a review, at a total cost of $6 million.[16] The government reviewed 660,000 files at a cost of $6 million using contract lawyers to respond to a nonparty subpoena. The order denying the government's motion for cost-shifting was upheld by the appellate court.

The answer does not lie in modifying the system somewhat to employ cheap labor to do a manual review. Outsourcing to low-paid lawyers may still be employed, but it is not a viable long-term strategy. Outsourcing only works when combined with new systems and technologies, such as predictive coding, and only when properly supervised and performed by highly skilled professionals. The answer is not outsourcing. The answer is a whole new system for e-discovery.

CONCLUSION

The current linear, confrontative, one-dimensional, largely manual, costly, Bates stamp approach to discovery must be replaced with a cooperative, iterative, largely automated, predictive coding–based, proportionality cost-controlled, hash value approach.

---

[16] *In re* Fannie Mae Securities Litigation, 552 F.3d 814, (D.C. App. Jan. 6, 2009).

4

There Can Be No Justice Without Truth and No Truth Without Search

Justice is based on truth—on what really happened. That is a basic problem in law because facts are usually contested. Each side has their own story. The truth is out there, but it requires search to discover. Truth and justice thus depend on effective search.

Truth in the law includes objective, reliable facts that may be admitted as evidence in a trial. The testimony of witnesses is by nature inherently subjective. Testimony alone is an unreliable path to truth. The discovery of objective facts is often dependent on the discovery of the writings made at the time by the people involved. Testimony taken later in legal proceedings—no matter how solemn the oaths—is filled with half-truths and, all too often, outright lies. Justice based on witness testimony alone is haphazard at best. The judge and jury must guess at who is lying. They are susceptible to lies, clever arguments, false hunches, publicity, and political pressures.

Judges and juries today often do not see the key writings they need to do justice. The fault lies with the lawyers who, in the U.S. system, are the ones charged with the duty to discover the truth. They often fail in this duty—not for want of trying, but for the difficulty in finding the key documents. The evidence is lost in plain view and the signal is lost in the noise—hidden by too much data. In many (perhaps even most) lawsuits today, legal search efforts are neither effective nor affordable. Therefore, our system of justice is in danger because justice depends on truth and truth on legal search.

This is my core belief after a lifetime as a lawyer. Therefore, despite the humor I try to evoke in my writings, I am dead serious, obsessed, and determined to change the way my profession goes about searching for evidence. That is why I now teach predictive coding methods on a regular basis, perform searches for clients, research various predictive coding methods, and have written more than 60 articles on predictive coding since 2012. (The complete list of these articles can be found at my law blog at *www.e-DiscoveryTeam.com.*)

EMPOWERING LAWYERS WITH THE TECHNOLOGY NEEDED TO FIND THE TRUTH

The advanced predictive coding software and methodologies now coming to light empower lawyers to save our system of justice from the flood of irrelevant information. We now carry around too much information, especially in large organizations, which typically keep more information in their computers than the largest libraries in the world. This sea of data unintentionally hides the few documents needed for the truth to be revealed in many lawsuits. That leaves many feeling frustrated, either as falsely accused or falsely denied. Either way, they are harmed and aggrieved by another, yet without a remedy in the courts.

HIDDEN IN PLAIN VIEW

The truth we need to resolve disputes is often hidden, lost in plain view among trillions of other bits of data and only accessible, if at all, by great expense or luck. When forced to resolve disputes on the basis of bad information—without the benefit of *the truth, the whole truth, and nothing but the truth*—justice is denied. We cannot survive for long as a civilization without justice; it is the glue that holds our society together. An unjust society will not stand.

TECHNOLOGY GOT US INTO THIS MESS; TECHNOLOGY CAN GET US OUT

Predictive coding and machine learning, *when used properly*, empower lawyers to save our legal system from information noise. For the past decade, the nearly insoluble problem of evidence retrieval has gotten worse every year. The evidence needed to do justice in an effective and affordable manner cannot be found because there is too much information. However, the tide is turning. This problem was brought on by unprecedented, rapid advances in computer technology. Computers got our system of justice into this mess; now, finally, computers can help us get out.

LAW AS A CALLING

A core belief of mine is that there is a direct connection between truth and justice—between truth and search. This is not based on supposition or theory, but on a lifetime of service as a lawyer. I have seen all too clearly the growing disconnect between the resolution of cases on merit with the full disclosure of the truth and settlements based on incomplete disclosures and costs.

It is no wonder that trials are disappearing, that cynicism and distrust are so widespread. It is no wonder that the guilty often go free and the innocent are convicted. It is no wonder that more and more misguided people take crazed notions of justice into their own hands. Justice is not a game. It is an important and dead serious cornerstone of the American way of life.

Law is a calling and a profession, not a job. Our work is about justice and truth. Join me in helping the profession to get through this technological crisis. Spend the time needed to master new technologies and share what you learn for the betterment of the profession and of the world. Reading this book is a good start, but I encourage you to go on and read my complex, recent works on legal search. They can be found online with links from my blog at *www.e-DiscoveryTeam.com.*

5 New Methods for Legal Search and Review

New systems of e-discovery are emerging that are designed for today's digital world. Unlike most existing e-discovery systems, they are not mere adaptations of old paper discovery ways. The new methods use an entirely new collaborative approach and technologies, exemplified by predictive coding software. Although this paradigm shift in discovery is just starting, many of the contours of the new methods are already apparent.

To repeat my prior conclusion, we are, in general terms, coming to realize that the current linear, confrontative, one-dimensional, largely manual, Bates stamp approach to discovery must be replaced with a multidimensional, cooperative, iterative, largely automated, hash value approach. Computers, advanced technologies, and communication systems created this problem for the law. They can now provide the solution. As the influential Sedona Conference put it:

> A consensus is forming in the legal community that human review of documents in discovery is expensive, time consuming, and error-prone. There is growing consensus that the application of linguistic and mathematic-based content analysis, search and retrieval technologies, and tools,

> techniques and process in support of the review function can effectively reduce the cost, time, and error rates.[1]

Attorneys are beginning to embrace new technologies as indispensable tools around which new legal processes and procedures are built. They understand that expensive human review must be significantly curtailed and redirected to the use of new software tools, not just keyword searching. The new tools include context and conceptual search software, advanced multidimensional indexing, and other new types of artificial intelligence–based predictive coding search and review programs.[2]

Technology should not be mistaken as an end in itself or a magic panacea. New software and other technology that is just plugged into the old paper search-and-review methods and processes—and old attitudes—is not the answer. A more fundamental change in legal practice is required. Quoting again from another important Sedona Conference commentary:

> The legal profession is at a crossroads: the choice is between continuing to conduct discovery as it has "always been practiced" in a paper world—before the advent of computers, the Internet, and the exponential growth of electronically stored information (ESI)—or, alternatively, embracing new ways of thinking in today's digital world. Cost-conscious clients and over-burdened judges are demanding that parties now undertake new approaches to solving litigation problems.[3]

Many of our leading jurists, information scientists, academics, scholars, writers, and legal practitioners recognize that the old methods

---

[1] *The Sedona Conference Best Practices Commentary on the Use of Search & Information Retrieval Methods in E-Discovery*, 8 SEDONA CONF. J. 189, 215 (2007).

[2] *See, e.g.*, Kevin D. Ashley & Will Bridewell, *Emerging AI+Law Approaches to Automating Analysis and Retrieval of ESI in Discovery Proceedings*, ICAIL Global E-Discovery/E-Disclosure Workshop (2009).

[3] George L. Baron & Jason R. Burke, *The Sedona Conference® Commentary on Achieving Quality in the E-Discovery Process, Executive Summary* (May 2009).

and attitudes that worked for paper no longer work for ESI.[4] Moreover, scientific research has shown that keyword search alone is ineffective and multimodal approaches that use keyword and other methods work far better.

The new legal methods for search and review take advantage of the computational properties of ESI. These new methods are not only tolerated by judges—they are encouraged because judges understand that they allow a way out of the unnecessary disputes and expenses that the old methods perpetuate. The new methods and technologies were also encouraged in a congressional action amending the Federal Rules of Evidence to include new Rule 502 on the protection of privileged information from inadvertent disclosure, which is a significant problem because of the high volumes of ESI to review. The rule sometimes requires a producing party to take reasonable steps to protect privilege. The Advisory Committee Notes to Federal Rule of Evidence 502 state the following:

> [A] party that uses advanced analytical software applications and linguistic tools in screening for privilege and work product may be found to have taken "reasonable steps" to prevent inadvertent disclosure.
>
> In addition, Principle 11 of *the Sedona Principles* (2007) states:
>
> A responding party may satisfy its good faith obligation to preserve and produce relevant electronically stored information by using electronic tools and processes, such as data sampling, searching, or the use of selection criteria, to identify data reasonably likely to contain relevant information.

---

[4]Victor Stanley, Inc. v. Creative Pipe, Inc., 250 F.R.D. 251 (D. Md. 2008) (Judge Grimm); Securities and Exchange Commission v. Collins & Aikman Corp., 2009 WL 94311 (S.D.N.Y. 2009) (Judge Scheindlin); Disability Rights Council of Greater Wash. v. Wash. Metro. Area Transit Auth., 2007 WL 1585452 (D.D.C. 2007) (Judge Facciola); United States v. O'Keefe, 2008 WL 449729 (D.D.C. 2008) (Judge Facciola); William A. Gross Const. Associates, Inc. v. American Mfrs. Mut. Ins. Co., _F.R.D._, 2009 WL 724954 (S.D.N.Y. 2009) (Judge Peck); Digicel (St. Lucia) Ltd & Ors v. Cable & Wireless & Ors, [2008] EWHC 2522 (Ch) (Justice Morgan) (UK decision).

Software has advanced to the point that computer review alone is at least as accurate as manual review, the so-called gold standard, and is getting better all of the time.[5] Furthermore, highly focused, multiple-phase production is becoming an accepted best practice, replacing the old paper methods of trying to discover all possible relevant writings in a single, broad, boilerplate request and production.[6] The profession is beginning to understand that in today's world of too much information, the production of *all* relevant information is a practical impossibility:

> The more information there is to discover, the more expensive it is to discover all the relevant information until, in the end, "discovery is not just about uncovering the truth, but also about how much of the truth the parties can afford to disinter."[7]

Instead, the goal should be production of as many highly relevant documents as is proportionate to the value and significance of the case:

> When balancing the cost, burden, and need for electronically stored information, courts and parties should apply the proportionality standard embodied in Fed. R. Civ. P. 26(b)(2)(C) and its state equivalents, which require consideration of the technological feasibility and realistic costs of preserving, retrieving, reviewing, and producing electronically stored information,

[5]Maura R. Grossman & Gordon v. Cormack, *Technology-Assisted Review in E-Discovery Can Be More Effective and More Efficient Than Exhaustive Manual Review*, RICH. J.L. & TECH. (Spring 2011), at 48; Herbert L. Roitblat, Anne Kershaw & Patrick Oot, *Document Categorization in Legal Electronic Discovery: Computer Classification vs. Manual Review* (Electronic Discovery Institute 2009).
[6]Covad Communications Co. v. Revonet Inc., 2008 WL 5377698 (D.D.C. 2008) (boilerplate paper forms still used to request ESI); Shannon Capone Kirk & Kristin Ali, *The Need for Art and Surgery in Discovery*, ELECTRONIC DISCOVERY (Ralph Losey ed., West 2010).
[7]*See, e.g.*, Rowe Entm't, Inc. v. William Morris Agency, Inc., 205 F.R.D. 421, 423 (S.D.N.Y. 2002).

as well as the nature of the litigation and the amount in controversy.[8]

The new discovery methods rely heavily upon various types of sampling and other metric-based quality control systems. Rule 34(a)(1) of the Federal Rules of Civil Procedure specifically allows sampling as a form of discovery. The official rules commentary confirms that this provision is intended to cover ESI as well as tangible objects.[9] Also consider the opinion of *Kipperman v. Onex Corp.*, 260 F.R.D. 682 (N.D. Ga. 2009). The court required production of "sample" backup tapes to weigh the volume and importance of the information on the tapes against the costs of their restoration and production before deciding whether to permit additional discovery. After reviewing the results of the sample, the court held that the ESI contained on the tapes was highly relevant and so compelled further discovery: "I don't ... declare these to be smoking guns but they certainly are hot and they certainly do smell like they have been discharged lately."[10]

---

[8]Rule 26(b)(2)(c) of the Federal Rules of Civil Procedure; *Sedona Conference Commentary on Proportionality* (2010); *The Sedona Principles* (2007), 2d Principle. *Also see Final Report on the Joint Project of the American College of Trial Lawyers and the Institute for the Advancement of the American Legal System* (2009) at 7 ("Proportionality should be the most important principle applied to all discovery.").
[9]*Also see In re* Vioxx Products Liability Litigation, No. 06-30378, 06-30379 2006 W 1726675, at *2 n.5 (5th Cir. May 26, 2006) ("By random sampling, we mean adhering to a statistically sound protocol for sampling documents."); *In re* Seroquel Products Liability Litigation, 244 F.R.D. 650 (M.D. Fla. 2007) ("Common sense dictates that sampling and other quality assurance techniques must be employed to meet requirements of completeness."); Mt. Hawley Ins. Co. v. Felman Production, Inc., 2010 WL 1990555 (S.D. W. Va. May 18, 2010) (plaintiff's attorney client privilege was lost because the plaintiff "failed to perform critical quality control sampling to determine whether their production was appropriate and neither over-inclusive nor under-inclusive."); McPeek v. Ashcroft, 202 F.R.D. 31, 34 (D.D.C. 2001) (ordering initial limited search of backup tapes within dates determined to be most relevant, as a "rational starting point" for ESI search).
[10]*Id.* at 691.

NEW COOPERATIVE STRATEGIES TO LITIGATION DISCOVERY

The new discovery methods should be based upon open communications and sharing of information of preliminary findings with the requesting party. This is what George Paul and Jason Baron called "virtuous cycle iterative feedback loops."[11] The parties need to exchange expert views and gain a common understanding of the relevant parameters. Scientific investigations on the effectiveness of search and review processes performed by the Text Retrieval Conference (TREC) Legal Track confirm this.[12] Studies also confirm that at least one meeting between opposing counsel to share initial review results, as well as to consider alterations based on mutual disclosure and input, significantly increases the overall precision and recall of the project.[13]

For this new system of open, iterative communication processes to work, lawyers must change their attitudes. The total adversarial approach to discovery, which is now prevalent in the United States, must be replaced by strategic cooperation with active judicial management where required. This is critical for the new iterative open process to work at maximum efficiency.

Cooperative discovery processes have long been required by the rules of professional ethics and procedure, but they were frequently misunderstood or ignored by attorneys succumbing to economic pressures to win at all costs.[14] They were also not well understood or

---

[11] *Information Inflation: Can the Legal System Adapt? Supra* at 32–36.

[12] Douglas W. Oard, Bruce Hedin, Stephen Tomlinson, & Jason R. Baron, Overview of the TREC 2008 Legal Track. In The Seventeenth Text Retrieval Conference. National Institutes of Standards and Technology, November 2008. Available at: *http://trec.nist.gov*. F.C. Zhao, D.W. Oard, and J.R. Baron, Improving Search Effectiveness in the Legal E-Discovery Process Using Relevance Feedback (paper presented at the DESI III Global E-Discovery/E-Disclosure Workshop at the 12th International Conference on Artificial Intelligence and Law, 2009).

[13] Jason R. Baron, Douglas W. Oard & Feng C. Zhao, *Improving Search Effectiveness in the Legal E-Discovery Process Using Relevance Feedback.*

[14] Ralph C. Losey, *Lawyers Behaving Badly*, 60 MERCER L. REV. 983 (Spring 2009).

enforced by the courts.[15] However, this has changed with recent scholarship and experiences showing the importance of cooperation in e-discovery.[16] Experience has shown that an overcontentious approach to discovery is a significant cause of many of the inflated costs of e-discovery. A strong movement is now underway in the United States to adopt a cooperative approach to discovery, being led by the Sedona Conference and more than 200 prominent judges and many more legal practitioners.[17] As Jason R. Baron, the past co-chair of the Sedona Conference Working Group on Electronic Document Retention and Production, explained:

> [T]he challenge is how best to reasonably (not perfectly) manage the exponentially growing amount of ESI caught in, and subject to, modern-day discovery practice. The answer lies principally in culture change (i.e., fostering cooperation strategies), combined with savvier exploitation of a range of sophisticated software and analytical techniques.[18]

CONCLUSION

Discovery of evidence and the legal analysis of relevancy and privilege determinations are at the heart of our legal system. They are essential to the common law evidence-based system of justice. The methods and tools used in paper discovery do not work with the vast stores of digital information ubiquitous in the 21st century. Therefore, e-discovery became expensive and riddled with mistakes; completely new methods

---

[15] Mancia v. Mayflower Textile Services. Co., 253 F.R.D. 354 (D.Md. Oct. 15, 2008).

[16] *The Case for Cooperation,* 10 SEDONA CONF. J. 339 (2009 Supp.) (Preface by Justice Breyer; lead article by Sedona Conference Working Group, edited by Bill Butterfield, Richard Braman, Ken Withers and others); *The Bull's-Eye View of Cooperation in Discovery,* 10 SEDONA CONF. J. 363 (2009 Supp.) (Professor Steven S. Gensler); Ralph Losey, *Mancia v. Mayflower Begins a Pilgrimage to the New World of Cooperation,* 10 SEDONA CONF. J. 377 (2009 Supp.).

[17] *See Sedona Cooperation Proclamation*, SEDONA CONF. (2008).

[18] Jason Baron, *Law in the Age of Exabytes,* XVII RICH. J.L. & TECH. 9, at 5 (2011).

and tools emerged for digital discovery and have finally caught on. The last impediment of *no judicial approval* has been destroyed. The way is now clear. The old linear method of reading all papers is being replaced by iterative methods that include predictive coding. The new ways involve cooperative, multidimensional, cyclic approaches that focus on proportional, phased productions.

The stated goal of the new legal processes has also changed. The goal is now legally adequate recall, not complete recall. It is discovery of all highly relevant information, but not necessarily all relevant information. Adequacy is determined on a case-by-case basis as necessary to render justice and, at the same time, not unfairly burden the parties to litigation. It is based on reasonability and proportionality, not a delusional notion of perfection that, in fact, has never been required by the law. The leaders in e-discovery have already made this change and are embracing and refining these new methods. They are managers of complex technologies and iterative quality control processes. They lead an e-discovery team. This trend will continue because it works. It saves money and mitigates risks.

The old-school, linear, confrontative, one-dimensional, largely manual, Bates stamp approach to e-discovery has already been abandoned by the top experts in the field. The new methods are multidimensional, cooperative, iterative, and include predictive coding as part of a multimodal approach. Predictive coding software works and, if it is properly used with the new legal methods, will be accepted by courts. The time to employ these new methods is now. You have nothing to lose but high expense and low recall.

As the famous Indian lawyer turned saint, Mahatma Gandhi, once said, “Be the change that you wish to see in the world.”

6

The 2015 e-Discovery FRCP Rule Amendments Begin a New Era of Proportional Discovery

This chapter presents a summary, analysis, and personal editorial on the 2015 amendments to the Federal Rules of Civil Procedure (FRCP) that pertain to electronic discovery. The new rules went into effect on December 1, 2015. They solidify and expand upon two important policies to e-discovery: proportionality and cooperation. They also clarify the rules on sanctions for spoliation by a complete rewrite of Rule 37(e).

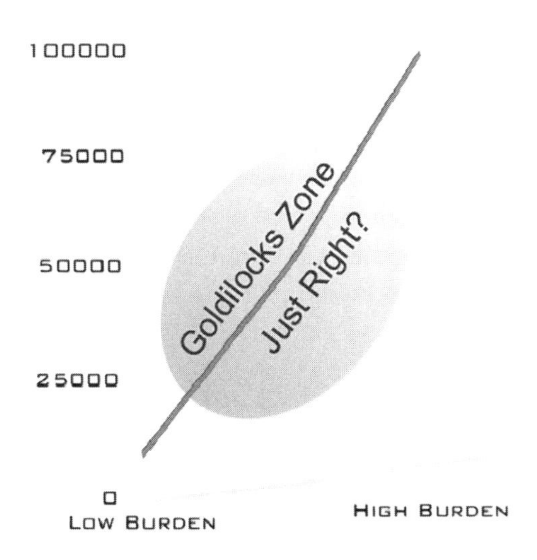

OVERALL IMPRESSIONS

The doctrines of proportionality and cooperation were already well embedded in the pre-2015 rules. For this reason, some argued that the rewording of Rules 1 and 26 in the 2015 amendments was not needed. My experience since December 2015 suggests that these clarifications are in fact very helpful, especially to general litigation attorneys and judges with no special expertise in e-discovery. For more experienced practitioners, the amendments may not have had as great of an impact on their practice because the doctrines of proportionality and cooperation were already being followed by them through interpretation of the old rules.[1] This interpretation was made much easier by the amendments, so even specialists are welcoming the change. The rule revisions make it a little easier for everyone to explain proportionality and cooperation positions to opposing counsel and the court. These rule amendments were written for the vast majority of U.S. lawyers struggling to do discovery in the modern age. Our profession remains embarrassingly computer challenged, so these rule revisions are a necessary and good thing.

My only regret concerning the rule amendments is that new Rule 37(e) may make it a little more difficult to catch and punish the few bad guys out there who try to cheat by destroying evidence. Still, we will get them. Fraudsters are never as smart as they think they are. When judges get the drift of what is happening, they will work around the vagueness in new Rule 37(e). Experienced federal judges can sniff out fraud a mile away and they do not hesitate to sanction bad-faith attempts to game the system.[2] Many spoliating parties were defeated under the old rules, so I am confident that this will continue under the new rules. The protests of some commentators and judges on this issue seem a bit

---

[1] *See, e.g.,* Mancia v. Mayflower Textile Services. Co., 253 F.R.D. 354 (2008) (J. Grimm); Ralph Losey, *Mancia v. Mayflower Begins a Pilgrimage to the New World of Cooperation*, 10 Sedona Conf. J. 377 (2009 Supp.); Ralph Losey, *Predictive Coding and the Proportionality Doctrine: A Marriage Made in Big Data*, 26 Regent U. Law Review 1 (2014).

[2] *See, e.g.*, Victor Stanley, Inc. v. Creative Pipe, Inc., 250 F.R.D. 251, 260, 262 (D.Md. 2008) (J. Grimm).

overstated to me, although I do agree that the new wording of new Rule 37(e) could be improved.

AN OVERLY HARD-FOUGHT VICTORY FOR PROPORTIONALITY

According to several long-time observers of the Rules Committee who I have spoken to, the 2015 FRCP rules amendments were the most politicized and hard-fought in history. e-Discovery was the focus of almost all the battles. (Other changes are not controversial, not really that important, and will not be addressed here.) Large corporate and plaintiffs' attorney groups lobbied the Rules Committee for years. Many believe that the well-funded defense bar largely won. Still, there is no doubt that the plaintiffs' bar retained some bite and won several small victories. It was classic lobbying at its worst by both sides.

As a result of the contentiousness of the proceedings, the final wording of some of the rules revisions are far from ideal. The language is a compromise. Years of interpretation and litigation seem assured. Perhaps that can never be avoided in FRCP amendments, but certainly a better job could have been done by scholars working above the fray.

PROPORTIONALITY DOCTRINE AND THE BEGINNING OF THE GOLDILOCKS ERA

In spite of the sordid background, two high-minded themes emerged. The primary theme of all of the amendments is *proportionality*. The secondary theme is an attempt to further attorney *cooperation* by communication. These two doctrines were promoted by the late, great founder of the Sedona Conference, Richard Braman.

The victory of proportionality proponents, myself included, may well usher in a new Goldilocks era for the bar. Everyone who reads the rules will know that they must look for discovery that is not too big, and not too small, but is just right. The *just right* zone of permitted discovery will balance out well-worn considerations, including costs, which are outlined by the rules. This is not really new, of course. Old Rule 26(b)(2)(C) had the same intent for decades to avoid undue burden by balance with benefits. Now, however, the proportionality concerns to avoid undue expenses for discovery are front and center for all discovery disputes. This forces judges to be more cost conscious and to not allow liberal discovery—regardless of costs, delays, and other burdens. I have been promoting the proportionality doctrine at the heart of these amendments since at least 2010, as did Richard Braman and the Sedona Conference. I recommend their *Commentary on Proportionality in Electronic Discovery* (2013), which can be downloaded without cost from the Sedona Conference website.[3]

Before the amendments went into effect in December 2015, only a few experts contended that the changes in the rules embodying proportionality would make a big difference. Some long-term observers said that there are no real changes at all. It was just window dressing, so nothing would change. Experiences since December 2015 suggest that the truth is somewhere in the middle, but slightly more inclined toward the "big change" side. The 2015 amendments appear to be helping all fair-minded attorneys to better serve their clients by protecting them from undue burdens in discovery, as well as from undue burdens in preservation.

We will all be arguing about the Goldilocks zone now, where the burden is *just right,* is proportional, and considers the criteria stated in the rules and the facts of the case. A one-size-fits-all approach is a thing of the past, especially when the one size is to save everything and produce everything. Papa Bear's big chair is way too large for most cases. Small chair or not, every litigant is entitled to a seat at the discovery table—even a trespasser like Goldilocks.

NEW RULE 26(B)(1): DISCOVERY SCOPE AND LIMITS

This section presents the new language of Rule 26(b)(1), which serves as the key provision in the 2015 amendments implementing proportionality. I have added boldface text and bullet points for clarity of reference. The original text of the rules is, as usual, just one long run-on sentence.

---

[3] *https://thesedonaconference.org/download-pub/1778. Also see* Ralph Losey, *Predictive Coding and the Proportionality Doctrine: A Marriage Made in Big Data*, 26 Regent U. Law Review 1 (2014) (this can be found online at my law blog *www.e-DiscoveryTeam.com*).

Parties may obtain discovery regarding any nonprivileged matter that is relevant to any party's claim or defense and proportional to the needs of the case, considering the following:

- The importance of the issues at stake in the action
- The amount in controversy
- The parties' relative access to relevant information
- The parties' resources
- The importance of the discovery in resolving the issues
- Whether the burden or expense of the proposed discovery outweighs its likely benefit

Information within this scope of discovery need not be admissible in evidence to be discoverable.

The first big change to Rule 26(b)(1) is not seen here because it is an omission. The scope is now limited to "any party's claim or defense." Previously a court could expand the relevance scope to "subject matter" of the case, not just specific claims. This expansion was supposed to require a good cause showing; however, in practice, the condition was given little weight by judges and was poorly understood by the bar. Full subject matter discovery was commonly allowed with little or no real showing of cause. Often, responding parties would simply capitulate and not demand a good cause showing. This could, in my experience, often lead to greatly expanded discovery. Now, relevance cannot be expanded beyond actual claims made. This is a big improvement.

I am proud to say that I suggested this revision to the Committee for adoption. I accomplished this without lobbying. I updated my prior blog on the proposal, added some more legal citations and analysis to make it more scholarly, and put forth my best argument.[4] That's it—I wrote a 3,700-word article and nothing more. I assumed the Committee would at least know about the article and maybe some of my regular visitors would read it. Because the proposal had merit, as far as I was concerned, the article was all that was required—no politics, no lobbying, just the submission of an article making my case for elimination of

---

[4] *Rethinking Relevancy: A Call to Change the Rules to Narrow the Scope of ESI Relevance* (e-Discovery Team, January 24, 2011).

subject matter discovery. That is how it should work. I was completely surprised to see the elimination of the old subject matter provisions when an early draft was published by the Rules Committee. All the Committee note says about this change is as follows:

> The amendment deletes the former provision authorizing the court, for good cause, to order discovery of any matter relevant to the subject matter involved in the action. Proportional discovery relevant to any party's claim or defense suffices. Such discovery may support amendment of the pleadings to add a new claim or defense that affects the scope of discovery.

The attention and politics of the Committee were focused on the *new* wording added to Rule 26(b)(1), which outlined the aforementioned six criteria for determining proportionality. Note that none of this language is new at all. The Committee used the exact same language that appeared in Rule 26(b)(2)(C) and then included the parties' relative access to relevant information as a last-minute addition. This added the accessibility provision already in Rule 26(b)(2)(B) from the 2006 rule amendments. Many had hoped that the Committee would improve the language to give the bench and bar more guidance. Still, the importance of the proportionality requirement was intended to be elevated by this move to a defined scope of relevance section, where discoverability is limited to information that is proportional to the needs of the case. This move is working as the Committee had hoped thus far.

The official 2015 Rules Committee Amendment Commentary explained the revision:

> The considerations that bear on proportionality are moved from present Rule 26(b)(2)(C)(iii). Although the considerations are familiar, and have measured the court's duty to limit the frequency or extent of discovery, the change incorporates them into the scope of discovery that must be observed by the parties without court order.

In most cases, but certainly not all, the main factor that comes into play is expense. Does the burden or expense of the proposed discovery outweigh its likely benefit? Also, what is the real, noninflated amount in controversy? The proportionality labeled rules now force a shift in thinking. They try to get the bench and bar to look at discovery as the tradeoff that it has always been and to get everyone thinking proportionally.

The final relevant change to Rule 26(b)(1) already seems to be widely misunderstood by the bar—namely, the rewording of provisions in the rule pertaining to discovery and admissibility. The old rule, which many lawyers disliked for good reason, said: "Relevant information need not be admissible at the trial if the discovery appears reasonably calculated to lead to the discovery of admissible evidence." It is true that this sentence was deleted, but it is *not* true that discovery is limited to admissible evidence. I have already seen at least one continuing legal education (CLE) course (sponsored by the American Bar Association) that incorrectly states that the old standard is dead. It is not. It is weakened, perhaps, but not gone. Remember, we are dealing with politics and compromise language. The plaintiffs' bar managed to keep the idea alive, but the sentence was modified and its placement was shuffled. Rule 26(b)(1) still says: "Information within this scope of discovery need not be admissible in evidence to be discoverable."

Here is how the Committee note explains this revision:

> The former provision for discovery of relevant but inadmissible information that appears reasonably calculated to lead to the discovery of admissible evidence is also amended. Discovery of nonprivileged information not admissible in evidence remains available so long as it is otherwise within the scope of discovery. Hearsay is a common illustration. The qualifying phrase—"if the discovery appears reasonably calculated to lead to the discovery of admissible evidence"—is omitted. Discovery of inadmissible information is limited to matter that is otherwise within the scope of discovery, namely that which is relevant to a party's claim or defense and proportional to the needs of the case. The discovery of inadmissible evidence should not extend beyond the permissible scope of discovery simply because it is "reasonably calculated" to lead to the discovery of admissible evidence.

I predict that lawyers will be litigating that subtle distinction for years. It remains to be seen what the magistrates who usually rule on such issues will make of this change. It also remains to be seen what the practical impact of this change will be. I think that the "claims made" versus "subject matter of the litigation" change will have a far greater impact.

WHAT IS A PROPORTIONAL SPEND ON E-DISCOVERY?

Assuming that monetary factors are the primary considerations in a case, how much should be spent on electronic discovery? Do not just brush the question aside by saying that every case is different. There are many similarities too. The longer you practice, the more aware you become of the recurring patterns. The Rules Committee wants the bench and bar to start thinking proportionally, from an overall budgetary perspective.

Consider the following hypothetical situation in which, all other factors being equal, money was the primary criteria to evaluate proportionality:

- Assume a case with a real-world true value of $1,000,000.
- What would be a proportional total cost of defense?
  - Assume $381,966 (38 percent).
- What would be a proportional total cost of all discoveries in such a case?
  - Assume $145,147 (14.6 percent).
- Now for the punch line, what would be a proportional cost of e-discovery in a case like that?
  - Assume $55,157 (5.6 percent).

Where am I getting these numbers? In part, I am getting these dollar amounts from my 35 years of experience as an attorney in private practice handling a wide variety of commercial and employment litigation cases (mainly large ones but also many smaller cases, and lately including thousands of employment law cases). These numbers may not hold true in single plaintiff discrimination cases or other small matters. However, there may be some general truth here. Most bar associations allow 40 percent recovery for fees in contingency cases, which compares with the 38 percent proportional expense assumed here: $381,966 in total fees and costs for a $1 million case. (Remember, you should assume true settlement value after weighing and discounting risks, not exaggerated positions or demands.)

What do you think? Is approximately 38 percent of the true case value a proportional total fee expense in complex litigation? Does 38 percent seem appropriate? What do you think is a proportional percentage for attorney fees?

What about my assumption of a total cost for all discovery of $145,147 in a case where the total fees are $381,966? Is it reasonable—proportional—to assume a cost of $145,147 for discovery of all types, including e-discovery? That number represents approximately 14.6 percent of the total amount in controversy. Is that number too low? Too high?

Going down to the last level, is it proportional to assume a cost of approximately 5.6 percent of the total amount in controversy for all e-discovery-related activities in a case? In this $1 million scenario, that rate would equate to $55,157. Again, what do you think? In a different but related question, what has your experience been? (Surveys have shown that a much higher percentage is common, especially in large cases like this hypothetical scenario.)

Now consider the bigger question: Does a general metric for the proportionality of expenditures to true case value make sense in the law—be it 38 percent or whatever? Assuming that it makes sense to talk of a general ratio for proportionality, is 6 percent of the total value of a case a reasonable amount for a party to pay for ESI discovery alone? If not, should it be higher or lower? What ranges are you seeing in practice? I am seeing a wide variety, but I think that is because we are still in an early stage of maturity; it should eventually settle down into a pattern.

Intel's in-house e-discovery counsel has reported at CLE events attended by the author that its e-discovery spending in large cases to average 80 percent of its total cost of defense. Therefore, if Intel spent $400,000 to defend a $1 million case, they would spend $320,000 on e-discovery—which is 32 percent of the total case value, not 6 percent. Does this seem fair? Appropriate? Proportional?

I can see patterns and cost ranges; at the same time, I see outliers in cost, especially on the high end. In my experience, these are usually due to external factors, such as extreme belligerence by one side or the other, attorney personality disorders, or intense spoliation issues. Sometimes, they may be associated with information management issues. However, if you discount the low and high outliers, a pattern starts to emerge.

CAN THE GOLDEN RATIO HELP US NAVIGATE THE GOLDILOCKS ZONE?

Aside from my experience with the cost of lawsuits and the experience of others, the primary source of the hypothetical numbers used here is from a famous ratio in math and art known as the golden ratio or golden mean: 1.61803399 to 1.0. I came up with the numbers in the hypothetical scenario by using this ratio:

$1,000,000 – $381,966 (38%) – $145,147 (14.6%) – $55,1567 (5.6%)

The numbers are progressively smaller by 0.3819661 percent, which follows the proportion of the golden ratio. The golden ratio is mathematically defined as the division where $a+b$ is to a as a is to b, as shown below. In other words, two quantities are in the golden ratio if the ratio of the sum of the quantities to the larger quantity is equal to the ratio of the larger quantity to the smaller one. In math, this is known as phi (Φ).

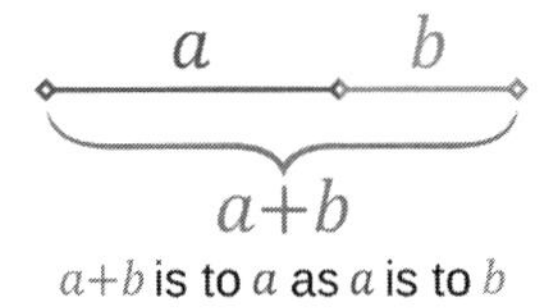

$a+b$ is to a as a is to b

It does not matter if the math confuses you. Just know that this proportion has been considered the perfect ratio to evoke feelings of beauty and contentment for thousands of years. It is well known in all of the arts, including painting, music, and architecture. It is the division that feels right, seems beautiful, and creates a deep intuitive sense of perfect division. It is still used today—just look at the designs of most Apple products. This ratio is also found everywhere in nature, including the human body and structure of galaxies. It seems to be hardwired into our brains and all of nature. There is far more to this than a math trick. The golden ratio seems to embody a basic truth. Every educated person should at least be familiar with this interesting phenomenon. If you have not heard of it yet, I suggest you check it out. Perhaps the idea of perfect proportionality in art, math, and science may also apply to law? Maybe it is a basic component of human reasonability and fairness? What do you think?

After giving a presentation much like this at a CLE course, I asked the question of whether the golden ratio in art, math, and science might also apply to the law. I wanted to know what everyone thought and to get some interaction going. It was a day-long conference dedicated solely to the topic of proportionality. Maura Grossman and I co-chaired the event in the fall of 2010, when the doctrine was still new. Everyone who attended (around 200 individuals) had a clicker and answered *yes* or *no* to the question. There was an eerie silence in the large auditorium after the results were quickly tabulated and shown on screen: 38 percent said *no* and 62 percent said *yes.* The golden ratio came through in the opinion of the 200 or so attorneys and judges in attendance. You cannot make this stuff up. At first, I thought maybe the technicians were messing with me, but no. It was automatic and they were not paying attention. It was real. It was beautiful.

A natural ratio clearly exists for proportionality in nature, art, and math. I am not saying that this 38/62 ratio, 1.61803399, also applies in the law as a general guide for proportionality—but it might. It is at least something to think about.

CHANGE TO RULE 37(E)

Rule 37(e) was completely rewritten and was the focus of most of the politics, which explains why the wording is such a mess. The Sedona Conference recommendations on how to revise the rules were largely ignored. A large part of the politics here, from what I could see, was to counteract recently retired Judge Shira Scheindlin (and a few other powerful judges, mostly in the Southern District of New York [SDNY]) who interpreted Second Circuit law to assert the right to impose case dispositive sanctions on the basis of gross negligence alone.[5] Many in the defense bar argued that there was a dangerous conflict in the circuits. However, because any large company can get sued in New York City, the SDNY views took practical priority over all conflicting views. They complained that the SDNY outlier views forced large corporations to overpreserve in a disproportionate manner. Naturally, Judge

[5] *See* Pension Committee of the University of Montreal Pension Plan v. Banc of America Securities, LLC, 685 F.Supp.2d 456, 465 (S.D.N.Y. 2010).

Scheindlin opposed these revisions and vigorously articulated the need to protect the judicial system from fraudsters. She proposed alternative language. The plaintiffs' bar stood behind her, but they lost. Sedona tried to moderate and failed for reasons I would rather not go into.

Other circuits outside of New York make clear that case dispositive sanctions should only be imposed if intentional or bad faith destruction of evidence was proven. Many defense bar types thought that this distinction with gross negligence was a big deal, so they fought hard and now pat themselves on the back. I think their celebration is overblown. I personally do not think the difference between bad faith and gross negligence is all that meaningful in practice. For that reason, I do not think that this rule change will have a big impact. Still, it is likely to make it somewhat easier for parties accused of spoliation to defend themselves and avoid sanctions, especially strong sanctions. If you think this is a good thing (I don't), then celebrate away. The reality is that this revision may well harm parties on both sides—defendants and plaintiffs alike. I know we now see many plaintiffs destroying evidence, especially cloud e-mails and Facebook posts. I expect they will rely upon this rule change to try to get away with it.

We will be litigating these issues for years. However, as mentioned, I have faith in our federal judiciary. No matter what the rules, if they sniff out fraud, they will take appropriate action. The exact wording of the rules will not matter much. What was once labeled as *gross negligence* will now be called *bad faith.* These concepts are so flexible and the entire pursuit of fraud like this is very fact intensive.

Let us examine Rule 37(e) in full, as it bears repetitive reading:

> If electronically stored information that should have been preserved in the anticipation or conduct of litigation is lost because a party failed to take reasonable steps to preserve it, and it cannot be restored or replaced through additional discovery, the court:
>
> (1) upon finding prejudice to another party from loss of the information, may order measures no greater than necessary to cure the prejudice; or

(2) only upon finding that the party acted with the intent to deprive another party of the information's use in the litigation may:
 (A) presume that the lost information was unfavorable to the party;
 (B) instruct the jury that it may or must presume the information was unfavorable to the party; or
 (C) dismiss the action or enter a default judgment.

The rule now makes proportionality expressly relevant to preservation for the first time. Before this change our primary authority was the order of the former Rules Committee chair, Judge Lee Rosenthal:

> Whether preservation or discovery conduct is acceptable in a case depends on what is reasonable, and that in turn depends on whether what was done—or not done—was proportional to that case and consistent with clearly established applicable standards.[6]

I strongly recommend that you read the extensive Committee note that tries to explain this rule. The notes can be cited and are often found to be persuasive; however, they are never technically binding authority. Still, until there is a body of case law on Rule 37(e), the notes will be very important.

MINOR CHANGES TO RULES 26 AND 34

Under Modified Rule 26(d)(2), a request for production (RFP) can be served any time after 21 days from the service of process. You do not have to wait for the 26(f) conference. Under Modified Rule 34(b)(2)(A), a response to an early RFP is not due until 30 days after the parties' first Rule 26(f) conference. This early service change was designed to encourage meaningful ESI discussion at 26(f) meet and greets.

Rule 34(b)(2)(B) was modified to require specific objections to request categories and "state whether any responsive materials are

[6]Rimkus v. Cammarata, 688 F. Supp. 2d 598 (S.D. Tex. 2010).

being withheld on the basis of that objection." Yet, as I have seen time and again, an objection is stated where no documents exist to begin with. Why? Rule 26(f) was modified to include discussion of preservation, as well as discussion of Evidence Rule 502 on clawback orders.

CHANGE TO RULE 16(B)

New language was added to Rule 16(b) as follows:

> Scheduling Order may …
> (iv) "… include any "agreements reached under Federal Rule of Evidence 502."
> (v) "direct that before moving for an order relating to discovery, the movant must request a conference with the court."

Everyone is encouraged to enter into clawback agreements and 502(d) orders.

CHANGE TO RULE 1.0: AN ALREADY GREAT, BUT UNDERUSED, RULE IS NOW EVEN BETTER

I saved the best rule change for last—the change to Rule 1.0. Judge Waxse (recently retired), the great promoter of Rule 1.0, should be happy. Rule 1.0 FRCP—the just, speedy, and inexpensive rule—is one of the most important rules in the book; yet, at the same time, it is one of the most overlooked and undercited. The 2015 amendments were designed to strengthen this important rule. Rule 1.0 has long required judges to "construe and administer" all of the other rules in such a way as to not only secure justice, as you would expect, but also to secure speedy and inexpensive determinations.

This dictate has long been an important policy for rule construction. It has been helpful to those who used it to oppose expensive, burdensome e-discovery. Nothing drives up expense more than "discovery about discovery" or detours into whether efforts to preserve, search, or produce ESI have been extensive enough. Courts may allow this kind of expensive discovery if justice requires it, but only after balancing the other two equally important considerations of speed and expense. Here we have another proportionality analysis—one that applies indirectly to every other rule in the book.

The 2015 amendments enlarged and strengthened the just, speedy, and inexpensive dictates by making it clear that this duty not only applies to the court and the judges, but also to the parties and their attorneys. Moreover, the revised rule not only requires judges and parties to construe and administer the rules to attain just, speedy, and inexpensive determinations, but it also requires them to employ all of the other rules in this manner.

The revised Rule 1.0 reads as follows (with new language in bold):

> They (all of the rules) should be construed, administered, **and employed** by the court **and the parties** to secure the just, speedy, and inexpensive determination of every action and proceeding.

These revisions squarely place the burden of efficient litigation upon counsel, as well as the court. It is now a clear rule violation for an attorney to demand justice, no matter what it costs or how long it takes. All three criteria must be considered and implemented. The change to Rule 1.0 perfectly frames all of the other 2015 amendments on proportionality and cooperation in ESI discovery and preservation. As the Rules Committee commentary to the Rule 1.0 amendments explains:

> Most lawyers and parties cooperate to achieve these ends. But discussions of ways to improve the administration of civil justice regularly include pleas to discourage overuse, misuse, and abuse of procedural tools that increase cost and result in delay. Effective advocacy is consistent with—and indeed depends upon—cooperative and proportional use of procedure.

Rule 1.0 now stands as a powerful shield to oppose any counsel's improper use of discovery as a weapon. Cost and delay must always be taken into consideration. Every motion for a protective order should begin with a recitation to Rule 1.0.

CONCLUSION

Update all of your discovery briefs to incorporate the new rules. Think proportional and act proportional. Sherlock Holmes was famous for his 7 percent solution; try mixing up your own 5.6 percent solution. Wouldn't it be beautiful to only spend $5,600 on e-discovery in a

$100,000 case? Most attorneys who perform any e-discovery end up spending far more than that.

Try to come up with an overall budget. Figure out what you think is proportional to the case. Do not wait to respond to excessive demands. Be proactive. How many custodians are proportional? What is an appropriate date range? What ESI is really important and necessary to the case? How many files need be reviewed under a realistic cost-benefit analysis? What are the benefits? What are the burdens?

Talk about true case value with opposing counsel. Never bad mouth your client, but be honest. Get beyond the bull and posturing that does nothing but cause delay and expense. That is the only way your proportionality discussions will get real and the only way the judge will ever see things your way.

What if the other side won't cooperate or you are dealing with inept phonies? Have these discussions with the judge. Ask for a 16(b) conference to work out disagreements that surface in the 26(f) conference. Most judges have a pretty good feel for what certain kinds of cases are usually worth. Have the wake-up call early and try to save your client money. Analyze and argue benefits and burdens. Also, be real and do not exaggerate what your e-discovery expenses will be. Back up your estimates with realistic numbers. Get vendors or specialists to help you.

All of this means that you must front-end your e-discovery work. It should come right after the retainer clears. The new Rule 37(e) is not a free pass to let up on preservation efforts or data collection. Find out what your problems are, if any, and talk about them as soon as possible. Bring them to the attention of the judge. Show that you are acting in good faith. The law never demands perfection, but it does demand honest and reasonable efforts.

Make your discovery plan early. What do you want the other side to produce? Be specific. Have concrete discussions at the 26(f) conference. The judges are getting fed up with drive-by meet and greets. It is dangerous to put off these discussions. Arrive at a fair balance between risk mitigation and cost control and move things along counsel. Speed counts, right up there with expense and justice. Your clients will appreciate that too.

Use honesty and diligence to navigate your way to the Goldilocks zone. Steer with realistic analysis. Be driven not only by the desire for justice, but also for quickness and sparse expense. Learn the new analytics, the new language, and concepts of proportion. Master these new rules, as well as the e-discovery rules that remain from the 2006 amendments, and you will prosper in the new Goldilocks Era.

7 Spilling the Beans on a "Secret" of Many Trial Lawyers

In this chapter, I'm going to spill the beans on a dirty little secret of the legal profession. This is a secret of trial lawyers—a large group in the tens, maybe hundreds, of thousands that I have been honored to be a part of since 1980. Their secret is already known by many but only spoken of by a few—usually judges who are accustomed to criticizing our kind.

Telling unflattering secrets is not exactly a way to win friends, but it may be a way to influence people. When unflattering things are brought to light and shine through the shrouds of denial, they have a way of effecting change. Sometimes the best love—the truest love—is tough love. Sometimes that is the quickest and best way to bring down the unhealthy walls of denial. Know the truth and the truth shall set you free. I do not expose these secrets to shame or embarrass my profession. I do so—and risk the wrath of some—because I care deeply about my profession. Popularity is overrated anyway. I would rather be an agent of change and teller of truth.

TRIAL LAWYERS' DIRTY LITTLE SECRET

The world has changed too quickly in the past few decades for most trial lawyers to keep up. As a result, most are unable to handle electronic evidence, including discovery of their clients' documents. A majority of trial lawyers are in complete denial of this incompetence. Others admit the painful truth but just bide their time until retirement. They hope that e-discovery will not pop up in any of their cases. If and when it does, they see nothing wrong with delegating core lawyer functions to outside vendors. Only a few admit the truth and have the intensity and dedication to do something about it—putting in the hard work to gain personal competence or (and this is just as good for those who have no aptitude or interest in e-discovery) bringing people into their firm who are competent and then having the wisdom to delegate to them.

The incompetence of most trial lawyers to do discovery is the secret that almost no one wants to talk about. Certainly, the vendors who sponsor most continuing legal education events have no incentive to do so; after all, they profit from this glaring competency gap. Some of the few people willing to speak up about it include Judge Facciola, Craig Ball, and me.[1] It is much easier to blame judges or the rules than your friends and colleagues.

The "secret" of incompetence is known by all specialists in the trade (although the word *incompetent* is rarely used). For instance, the ABA ethics specialists must know this well, considering their new Comment 8 to ABA Model Rule 1.1 that was added in 2012:[2]

> To maintain the requisite knowledge and skill, a lawyer should keep abreast of changes in the law and its practice, including the benefits and risks associated with relevant technology....

As of November 2015, 17 states had amended their rules to include this comment.

---

[1] *See, E-Discovery Competence Is a Fundamental Ethical Challenge Now Faced by the Legal Profession*, Chapter 34 of ELECTRONIC DISCOVERY (West 2010).

[2] Rimkus v. Cammarata, 688 F. Supp. 2d 598 (S.D. Tex. 2010).

The California Bar went a little further and issued a ruling, California Formal Opinion No. 2015-193.[3] Here is the California Bar's digest summarizing this important opinion:[4]

> An attorney's obligations under the ethical duty of competence evolve as new technologies develop and become integrated with the practice of law. Attorney competence related to litigation generally requires, among other things, and at a minimum, a basic understanding of, and facility with, issues relating to e-discovery, including the discovery of electronically stored information ("ESI"). On a case-by-case basis, the duty of competence may require a higher level of technical knowledge and ability, depending on the e-discovery issues involved in a matter, and the nature of the ESI. Competency may require even a highly experienced attorney to seek assistance in some litigation matters involving ESI. An attorney lacking the required competence for e-discovery issues has three options: (1) acquire sufficient learning and skill before performance is required; (2) associate with or consult technical consultants or competent counsel; or (3) decline the client representation. Lack of competence in e-discovery issues also may lead to an ethical violation of an attorney's duty of confidentiality.

California also went on to clarify that consulting with co-counsel or vendors does not relieve an attorney from his or her personal duty of competence. The exact wording is well worth study:

> The duty of competence in rule 3-110 includes the duty to supervise the work of subordinate attorneys and nonattorney employees or agents. See Discussion to rule 3-110. This duty to supervise can extend to outside vendors or contractors, and even to the client itself. *See* California State Bar Formal Opn. No. 2004-165 (duty to supervise outside contract lawyers);

[3]The State Bar of California Standing Committee on Professional Responsibility and Conduct, *Formal Opinion No. 2015-193, available at http://ethics.calbar.ca.gov/Portals/9/documents/Opinions/CAL%202015-193%20%5B11-0004%5D%20(06-30-15)%20-%20FINAL.pdf.*
[4]Rimkus v. Cammarata, 688 F. Supp. 2d 598 (S.D. Tex. 2010).

> San Diego County Bar Association Formal Opn. No. 2012-1 (duty to supervise clients relating to ESI, citing *Cardenas v. Dorel Juvenile Group, Inc.* (D. Kan. 2006) 2006 WL 1537394).
>
> Rule 3-110(C) permits an attorney to meet the duty of competence through association with another lawyer or consultation with an expert. *See* California State Bar Formal Opn. No. 2010-179. Such expert may be an outside vendor, a subordinate attorney, or even the client, if they possess the necessary expertise. **This consultation or association, however, does not absolve an attorney's obligation to supervise the work of the expert under rule 3-110, which is a non-delegable duty belonging to the attorney who is counsel in the litigation, and who remains the one primarily answerable to the court.** An attorney must maintain overall responsibility for the work of the expert he or she chooses, even if that expert is the client or someone employed by the client. The attorney must do so by remaining regularly engaged in the expert's work, by educating everyone involved in the e-discovery workup about the legal issues in the case, the factual matters impacting discovery, including witnesses and key evidentiary issues, the obligations around discovery imposed by the law or by the court, and of any relevant risks associated with the e-discovery tasks at hand. The attorney should issue appropriate instructions and guidance and, ultimately, conduct appropriate tests until satisfied that the attorney is meeting his ethical obligations prior to releasing ESI (emphasis added).

The competence issues can be seen by anyone who looks. For instance, a survey of attorneys found that e-discovery was only discussed in 30 percent of 26(f) conferences, which included discussions *not* to do e-discovery.[5] It is well known to all in the profession that lawyers are avoiding electronic discovery in droves, even though all of their clients have computers and store most of their information electronically. They ignore it because they do not know how to do it. It is like the story of the man looking for his door key underneath the lamp post on the sidewalk, even though he knows full well that he dropped

[5] Federal Judicial Center, *Case-Based Civil Rules Survey* (2009).

the key 20 feet away by the front door. He does not look for the key where he dropped it because he cannot see anything there. There is no light there. This little joke now applies to most of the trial lawyers in our profession today.

This knowledge gap is also the primary cause of most of the undue expense of e-discovery. This is yet another secret that few are willing to talk about, especially the vendor experts who, once again, profit from the inefficient overreview and excessive productions that now plague the industry.

WHY SO MANY TRIAL LAWYERS ARE UNABLE TO DO DISCOVERY

How did this come to pass? After all, trial lawyers today are just as smart—probably smarter—than the many generations of trial lawyers who came before them. They are also just as industrious. So, how did the competency gap in discovery come to pass?

Call me an enabler if you will, but I do not think it is their fault. These are my friends, my fellow trial lawyers. They are a good group. They are learned (perhaps too learned for their own good). They are victims of circumstance, society, schools, and academia. If anything, they are too literate. Law school attracts young men and women who are like that. The computer-phobic trial lawyers of today are the inevitable product of thousands of years of cultural heritage. Their current failings are perfectly understandable in view of the culture in which they grew up. Let me explain.

For millennia, all writings were on paper. From handwritten scrolls to the printed word, paper is deeply engrained in our culture and very souls. The more learned the person, the deeper the engraving is likely to be. For centuries, the legal profession has been dependent on writings (referred to in the law as *documents*) as the key evidence to resolve disputes. Although testimony by witnesses is often dramatic and important, all trial lawyers know that documentary proof is the real powerhouse in proving cases.[6]

---

[6] *See, e.g.,* Ralph Losey, *Mathematical Formula for Justice Proves the Importance of ESI in Civil Litigation*, Chapter 4 of ELECTRONIC DISCOVERY (West 2010).

Because paper writings are the foundation of all literary culture—indeed of all education in the civilized world—the paper form of documentary evidence is well known and easily mastered by every lawyer and judge. We are, after all, a learned profession, not just some trade. For that reason and because the number of relevant documents was usually few in number, paper discovery was always a relatively simple task that was usually delegated to starting lawyers. It worked in yesterday's world of paper—but that was yesterday. That world is going, or gone.

The paper basis of culture and evidence has changed in a historical blink of the eye. In just one generation, documents have dematerialized. They have transformed into a dizzying array of digital media. For instance, since April 2011, Amazon, the world's largest bookstore, has been selling more digital books than paper.[7] Documents originally created on paper still exist in our society, but they are growing rare.[8] Most of the paper documents we still see are merely printouts of one dimension (the text) of the original electronic information.

The law recognizes this transformation and the Federal Rules of Civil Procedure were amended in 2006 to include *electronically stored information* (ESI) as information that can be discovered and used as evidence in lawsuits.[9] ESI is not specifically defined in the rules. The Rules Committee commentary explained why:

> The wide variety of computer systems currently in use, and the rapidity of technological change, counsel against a limiting or precise definition of electronically stored information. Rule 34(a)(1) is expansive and includes any type of information that is stored electronically.[10]

---

[7]Claire Cain Miller & Julie Bosman, *E-Books Outsell Print Books at Amazon,* NY TIMES (May 9, 2011), *available at* http://www.nytimes.com/2011/05/20/technology/20amazon.html.

[8]Zubulake v. UBS Warburg LLC, 217 F.R.D. 309, (S.D.N.Y. 2003) (FN 5 cites Wendy R. Liebowitz, *Digital Discovery Starts to Work*, NAT'L L.J., Nov. 4, 2002, at 4, which reports that 93 percent of all information generated in 1999 was in digital form).

[9]Rule 34(a)(1), Federal Rules of Civil Procedure (2006).

[10]Rules Committee Commentary to the 2006 Amendments to Rule 34, Subdivision (a).

Even without specific amendments to rules, all courts today (state and federal) have treated ESI as potentially admissible evidence subject to discovery since at least the turn of the century. Nothing is new here, yet the incompetence continues.

Many see the change away from paper writings as a much more profound cultural revolution than that precipitated by Gutenberg, which took centuries to play out, not decades, and still maintained the same paper media. This rapid transformation is having a profound effect upon the law and lawyers. See, for instance, the important early essay by George Paul and Jason Baron.[11] The authors explained how writing co-evolved with civilization over the past 50 centuries or longer, with a slow but steady increase in information as writing technologies slowly improved. They point out that this all changed when humans invented a totally different form of electronic writing, free from physical confines, that triggered a Big Bang–like explosion of a new universe of virtually unlimited information. Paul and Baron predicted in 2007 that the legal profession would have to significantly change and adopt new strategies of practice to cope with this information revolution. I predict the same thing. In fact, I write now to try to push this change. How can the rest of the world change and the law not change with it? However, change does not come easy to the legal profession, and we are now witnessing a painful, slow, generational shift.

The changes in writing and the resulting information explosion brought about by rapid advances in computer technology are simply too much, too fast, for most lawyers today to handle. Not only is ESI changing and evolving into new forms every year, but it is now multiplying at an exponential rate that is almost beyond comprehension.[12]

---

[11] George L. Paul & Jason R. Baron, *Information Inflation: Can the Legal System Adapt*? 13 Rich. J.L. & Tech. 10 (2007).

[12] *See, e.g.*, Rowe Entm't, Inc. v. William Morris Agency, Inc., 205 F.R.D. 421, 429 (S.D.N.Y. 2002) (explaining that electronic data is so voluminous because, unlike paper documents, "the costs of storage are virtually nil. Information is retained not because it is expected to be used, but because there is no compelling reason to discard it"), *aff'd*, 2002 WL 975713 (S.D.N.Y. May 9, 2002); *Data, Data Everywhere* (The Economist, March 2010). *Also see* Jason Baron & Ralph Losey, *E-Discovery: Did You Know*? video at *https://www.youtube.com/watch?v=bWbJWcsPplM&list=FLiiIoqmOaKR28OqcBJaEQrQ*.

LAW SCHOOLS PERPETUATE THE PROBLEM

The secret known by many, but spoken by few, is that most lawyers today are unfamiliar with ESI and the complex systems that store it. They prefer the familiar paper and alphabetical filing cabinets. Unfortunately, most documentary evidence no longer lives there. You would think that law schools would come to the rescue and train the next generation of lawyers on ESI, but don't hold your breath on that one. As an adjunct law professor for years at the University of Florida—one of the few schools in the country that teaches e-discovery—I know first-hand how far we have to go. I also know that CLEs for post-graduate studies are not much better.

Even though many scholars, jurists, and practitioners recognize the problems created by the inability of most lawyers to keep pace with technology, most law schools still only train students in paper evidence and paper discovery. Students graduate unprepared to handle the ESI where the truth of past events is now stored.[13]

MORE REASONS LAWYERS FIND IT SO HARD TO ADAPT

The profession, including our law schools, is by nature slow to change. This is a conservative profession. The law was designed that way. It was designed to be a stabilizing force in society. The legal profession is slow to change on all fronts, but especially in technology areas. There are few Steve Jobs hippie-tech types in the field of law, much less Wozniak types. Most lawyers and judges are not technologically sophisticated. This reinforces their resistance to computer-based discovery. Even younger lawyers, who may have had much exposure to computers, are usually not

---

[13] *See, e.g.*, William Hamilton, *The E-Discovery Crisis: An Immediate Challenge to our Nation's Law Schools*, ELECTRONIC DISCOVERY (West 2010); Shannon Capone Kirk & Kristin G. Ali, *Teach Your Children Well: A Case for Teaching E-Discovery in Law Schools*, ELECTRONIC DISCOVERY (West 2010); Shira Scheindlin & Ralph Losey, *E-Discovery and Education*, ELECTRONIC DISCOVERY (West 2010); Ralph Losey, *Plato's Cave: Why Most Lawyers Love Paper and Hate e-Discovery and What This Means to the Future of Legal Education*, ELECTRONIC DISCOVERY (West 2010).

interested in them. Like their more senior attorneys, they are typically straight-laced liberal arts majors and only rarely have a science or engineering background, much less a truly creative background.

However, there is another less obvious reason that should also be understood. When documents first began to be created electronically in the 1980s and 1990s, most were essentially word-processing documents. Moreover, most of the key electronic evidence of any kind was printed out and also existed in paper form. Thus, even though the original documents were electronic, they could still be found and presented as evidence using paper-based models.

This factor was well known and relied upon for years by trial lawyers resisting e-discovery. It was not necessary. You did not have to do it to adequately represent your clients. The reliance was acceptable in the 1990s, where the observation was true for most electronic evidence. It also survived with some efficacy in the early 2000s. But now, in the second decade of the 21st century, this is more myth than fact. The diversity of writings has expanded tremendously, especially Internet-based writings. Also, the habits of witnesses have changed, such that they no longer automatically print out electronic writings and file them away as paper. Yet, many still hold onto this notion and think that there is no harm to their clients by avoidance of e-discovery. They may even think they are helping their clients by avoiding unnecessary expenses.

Today, critical evidence is more often than not never printed out. It exists only as e-mail, text messages, spreadsheets, PowerPoints, Facebooks, Tweets, and the like. Therefore, the efficacy of paper-only discovery is rapidly disappearing. Attorneys who proceed without electronic discovery today will likely miss critical evidence. This situation worsens as the habits of witnesses change every year, with fewer and fewer relevant documents being printed out where "paper lawyers" can find them. They remain hidden in electronic form.

CONCLUSION

The secret has now been told, once again. Most lawyers are not able to handle electronic evidence. The lawyers who do know how to preserve and find electronic information have a distinct advantage over their technophobe colleagues. This advantage is growing every day.

Despite this unconverted fact, the primary coping mechanism of many trial lawyers remains avoidance and denial. That is where gadflies like me, Craig Ball, and Judge Facciola come in—to point out the obvious and chide them on. So too do the next generation of Young Turks, the twenty-something trial lawyers who know how to do e-discovery—and I mean *really* know how to do e-discovery and take advantage of others who don't. I hear the stories my students tell. The next generation of whiz kids are out there, shamelessly running circles around their elders—much to the delight of their clients.

Competition is a powerful motivator. Those who refuse to change and think they are safe in avoidance of e-discovery among their cronies may soon be in for a rude awakening. They may be fired. My Socratic method of bringing unwelcome news is actually far kinder than the ways of his student, Alexander. Twenty-five hundred years ago, when paper documents were still new, Alexander was offered the world. He conquered it ruthlessly. Socrates, who taught and paved the way for him, was offered poison wine. He drank it fearlessly with understanding beyond our ken.

I know that many lawyers and law firms do not like this message of incompetence and wish that e-discovery would just go away. They will be crushed with time and the next generation of lawyers, of that I have no doubt. They are victims of a paper culture that is vanishing before their eyes. To use the Socratic metaphor, I can only yell about the shadows of the flames, not make them see the sun.

Revealing the causes of lawyer technophobia may help lawyers to escape their paper chains. In summary, this chapter has talked about five fundamental causes of the problem of Luddite lawyers:

1. Historically unprecedented advances in technology engendered an explosion in the volume and complexity of written evidence.
2. The law is a learned profession and lawyers, more than most, are deeply entrenched in the past paper-based civilizations that are now vanishing before our eyes.
3. Elders in the profession are the ones who control the social mores and priority designations; they are more deeply immersed

in paper, and more detached from the new electronic worlds, than the new generation of lawyers now entering the field.

4. Law schools are very slow to recognize, much less meet, the educational challenges raised by the paradigm shift in evidence and discovery.
5. The legal profession is inherently conservative in nature. Most young people who are drawn to the profession do not have the kind of creative, artistic, or technical computer backgrounds needed to excel in the new technical paradigms and new team paradigms.

Until just a few years ago, you could still effectively represent your clients in most cases by relying on the paper printouts of original electronics. *Stalling and avoiding* real e-discovery tactics still worked, but this is no longer true. Facebook and other social media, when combined with the sheer volume of messages of all kinds, including e-mails and text messages, provided the final death blow to the continued use of these paper strategies.

8 Four Secrets of Legal Search

This chapter will reveal some of the secrets of legal electronically stored information (ESI) search experts. I am referring to the few technophiles, lawyers, and scientists in the e-discovery world who specialize in the search for relevant electronic evidence in large chaotic collections of ESI, such as e-mail. This exposé will include a secret deeply hidden in the shadows, known only by a few. Before I can get to the dark secret, I must lay bare a few other search secrets that are not so hidden.

A SECRET OF SEARCH ALREADY KNOWN TO MANY

You may have heard this first secret already, especially if you have read Judge Peck's famous opinion in *William A. Gross Construction Associates, Inc. v. American Manufacturers Mutual Insurance Co.*, 256 F.R.D. 134, 136 (S.D.N.Y. 2009). He repeated it again in his article *Predictive Coding: Reading the Judicial Tea Leaves* (LAW TECH. NEWS, Oct. 17, 2011). Despite these writings and many continuing legal education (CLE) courses on the subjects, many in the law still do not know these things, much less litigants or the public at large.

The wake-up call on search has a long way to go before it is a shot heard round the world. I am reminded of that on an almost-daily basis as I interact, usually indirectly, with opposing counsel in employment cases around the country. They often insist on antiquated search methods. They seem unaware of the many keyword search methods now available on good document review software—including the most advanced method, predictive coding. One of the leading jurists in this area, Judge Paul Grimm, gave a good general description of these alternatives to keyword search way back in 2008, even before the advent of review software with predictive coding features (now generally referred to as *concept searches* or *analytics*):

> In addition to keyword searches, other search and information retrieval methodologies include: probabilistic search models, including "Bayesian classifiers" (which searches by creating a formula based on values assigned to particular words based on their interrelationships, proximity, and frequency to establish a relevancy ranking that is applied to each document searched); "Fuzzy Search Models" (which attempt to refine a search beyond specific words, recognizing that words can have multiple forms. By identifying the "core" for a word the fuzzy search can retrieve documents containing all forms of the target word); "Clustering" searches (searches of documents by grouping them by similarity of content, for example, the presence of a series of same or similar words that are found in multiple documents); and "Concept and Categorization Tools" (search systems that rely on a thesaurus to capture documents which use alternative ways to express the same thought).[1]

---

[1]Victor Stanley, Inc. v. Creative Pipe, Inc., 250 F.R.D. 251 (D. Md. 2008) at FN 9 of the opinion. For more early opinions discussing alternatives to keyword search, *see* Securities and Exchange Commission v. Collins & Aikman Corp., 2009 WL 94311 (S.D.N.Y. 2009) (Judge Scheindlin); Disability Rights Council of Greater Wash. v. Wash. Metro. Area Transit Auth., 2007 WL 1585452 (D.D.C. 2007) (Judge Facciola); United States v. O'Keefe, 2008 WL 449729 (D.D.C. 2008) (Judge Facciola); Digicel (St. Lucia) Ltd & Ors v. Cable & Wireless & Ors, [2008] EWHC 2522 (Ch) (Justice Morgan) (UK decision).

THE FIRST *NOT-SO-SECRET* SECRET: KEYWORD SEARCH IS REMARKABLY INEFFECTIVE AT RECALL

First of all—and let me put this in very plain vernacular so that it will sink in—*keyword search sucks*. It does not work—that is, unless you consider a method that misses 80 percent of relevant evidence to be a successful method. Keyword search alone only catches 20 percent of relevant evidence in a large, complex data set, such as an e-mail collection. Yes, it works on Google, Lexis, and Westlaw, but it does not work well in the legal world of evidence gathering. Keyword search only provides reliable recall value when used as part of a multimodal process that uses other search methods and quality controls, such as iterative testing, sampling, and adjustments. It fails miserably when used in the context of blind guessing, which is the negotiated method still used by most lawyers today. I have written about this many times before and will not repeat it here again.[2]

Keyword Search Still Has a Place in Best Practices

Keyword search still has a place at the table of 21st century search, but only when used as part of a multimodal search package with other search tools and only when the multimodal search is used properly with iterative processes, real-time adjustments, testing, sampling, expert input and supervision, and other quality control procedures.

Proof of the Inadequacies of Keyword Search When Not Used as Part of a Multimodal Process

If you want scientific proof of the incompetence of keyword search alone when not used as part of a modern multimodal process, look at the landmark research on Boolean search by information scientists David Blair and M.E. Maron from 1985. The study involved a 40,000-document case (350,000 pages). The lawyers, who were experts in keyword search, estimated that the Boolean searches they ran

---

[2] *See, e.g.*, Ralph Losey, *Child's Game of "Go Fish" Is a Poor Model for e-Discovery Search*, ADVENTURES IN ELECTRONIC DISCOVERY (West 2011).

uncovered 75 percent of the relevant documents. In fact, they had only found 20 percent.[3] Delusion is a wonderful thing, isn't it?

Please join me in this Quixotic quest. Spread the word. We must all continue to tell the unpopular truth. Otherwise, we will live in a world of injustice where relevant evidence is lost in ESI skyscrapers of junk, where cases are decided on false testimony and whim. We have worked way too hard building our systems of justice over centuries to let a few billion terabytes of ESI destroy them—but they will be destroyed if we are complacent.

More recently, the National Institute of Standards and Technology Text Retrieval Conference (TREC) Legal Track confirmed that keyword search alone still finds only about 20 percent, on average, of relevant ESI in the search of a large data set. In batch tests of negotiated keyword terms, they did much worse. The Boolean searches had a mean precision ratio of 39 percent, but recall averaged less than 4 percent.[4] Yes, you read that right: The negotiated keywords missed 96 percent of the documents. I wonder how many times lawyers have done this in practice and never known it. Please note that this awful 4 percent recall came out of so-called batch tasks, in which there were no subject matter experts, testing, or appeals. These safeguards were present only in the interactive tasks. The batch tasks are thus like a Go Fish scenario, where people simply guess keywords blindly without testing, sampling, refining, or iterating.[5] The same research also shows that alternative multimodal methods do much better. These methods still use some keyword-based search tools, but they also use predictive coding and other artificial intelligence (AI) algorithms with seed-set iteration and sampling methodologies.

If you still want more proof, the final report on the 2010 TREC tests again confirmed our little secret on the absurd ineffectiveness of keyword

[3]David C. Blair & M.E. Maron, *An Evaluation of Retrieval Effectiveness for a Full-Text Document Retrieval System* (Communications of the ACM, March 1985).
[4]Hedlin, Tomlinson, Baron & Oard, *2009 TREC Legal Track Overview*, TREC legal track at §3.10.9.
[5]Losey, *supra*.

search alone.[6] The confirmation comes inadvertently from tests done by a fine team of information science graduate students from the Indian Statistical Institute, Kolkata, in West Bengal, India. The students participated in the 2010 TREC Legal Interactive task in Topic 301 and Topic 302. They performed what proved to be an interesting experiment, although for reasons other than what they intended. The Indian Statistical Institute had an AI predictive software coding tool using clustering techniques that they wanted to test. However, the software could not handle the high volumes of e-mail involved in the 2010 test (685,592 items), so the team had no choice but to cull down the amount of e-mail somewhat before they could use their software. For that reason, they decided to use keywords to cull down the corpus (a term that information scientists love to use) before running their AI clustering software. Here is their description of the process:[7]

> We attempted to apply DFR-BM25 ranking model on the TREC legal corpus. We chose Terrier 3.0 as this toolkit has most of the IR methods implemented within. But as we received the TREC legal data set we realized that it would be difficult to manage such a large volume of data. So, we decided to reduce the corpus size by Boolean retrieval. We chose Lemur 4.11 as it supports various useful Boolean query operators which would suit our purpose. On the set obtained from Boolean retrieval we decided to apply ranked retrieval techniques.... The use of Boolean retrieval

---

[6]National Institute of Standards and Technology (NIST) Special Publication SP 500-294. Papers presented at the Nineteenth Text Retrieval Conference (TREC 2010) Proceedings include: Gordon V. Cormack, Maura R. Grossman, Bruce Hedin, and Douglas W. Oard., *Overview of the TREC 2010 Legal Track*, http://trec.nist.gov/pubs/trec19/t19.proceedings.html; and Kripabandhu Ghosh, Swapan Kumar Parui, Prasenjit Majumder, Ayan Bandyopadhyay, and S. John J. Raja Singh., *Indian Statistical Institute, Kolkata at TREC 2010: Legal Interactive*, http://trec.nist.gov/pubs/trec19/papers/indian-stat-institute.LEGAL.pdf.

[7]National Institute of Standards and Technology (NIST) Special Publication SP 500-294. Kripabandhu Ghosh, Swapan Kumar Parui, Prasenjit Majumder, Ayan Bandyopadhyay, and S. John J. Raja Singh., *Indian Statistical Institute, Kolkata at TREC 2010: Legal Interactive*, http://trec.nist.gov/pubs/trec19/papers/indian-stat-institute.LEGAL.pdf. Paper presented at the Nineteenth Text Retrieval Conference (TREC 2010) Proceedings.

> has the disadvantage that it will limit further search to the documents retrieved at this stage and have an adverse effect on our recall performance. But it would scale down the huge corpus size considerably (see Table 1) and enable us to perform our experiments on a smaller set which would reduce processing time.

The use of keyword Boolean as an upfront filter turns out to have been a mistake, at least as far as any quest for good recall was concerned. Perhaps the students thought their keywords would be better than the lawyer-derived keywords in the famous Blair Maron study. I see this kind of mistake made by opposing counsel all of the time, who think their keywords are so good that they could not possibly miss 80 percent of all relevant documents in the corpus. They have an almost superstitious belief in the magical power of keywords and think that their Boolean is better that your Boolean. Hogwash! All untested keyword searches are relatively ineffective—no matter who you are, how many lawsuits you have won, or what Google sites you found.

The computer algorithms used in the 1985 Blair Maron test are essentially the same as those used today for keyword searches—pretty simple index matching and antiquated software. This works fine in academic settings with artificially controlled data sets or organized databases, but it does not survive contact with the real world where words and symbols are chaotic and vague, just like the people who create them. In real-world e-mail collections, the meaning of documents is hidden in subtle (and not-so-subtle) word and phrase variations, misspellings, abbreviations, slang, and obtusity. In reality, when large data sets are involved, no human is smart enough to guess the right keywords.

Getting back to the 2010 TREC study, in Topic 301, the use of Boolean retrieval allowed the scientists from India to reduce the initial corpus from 685,592 to 2,715. Then, they ran their sophisticated software on the whittled-down corpus. The final metrics must have been disappointing. The TREC judges found that their precision in Topic 301 was pretty good. It was 87 percent (meaning that 87 percent of the items retrieved were determined to be relevant after an appeal process). However, their recall was simply terrible at only 3 percent (meaning that their method failed to retrieve an estimated 97 percent of the relevant documents in the original 685,592 collection). Random guessing might have done as well in the recall department, maybe even in the F1 measure (the harmonic mean of precision and recall). In their other interactive task, Topic 302, the results were comparable. They attained a precision rate of 69 percent and a recall rate of 9 percent. Again, this means that the researchers left 91 percent of the relevant documents on the table and only managed to find 9 percent of the relevant documents.

THE SECOND SEARCH SECRET (KNOWN ONLY TO A FEW): THE GOLD STANDARD TO MEASURE REVIEW IS REALLY MADE OUT OF LEAD

The so-called gold standard used to judge recall and precision rates in information science studies is human review. This brings up an even more important secret of search—a subtle secret known only to a few. Experiments in TREC, which were conducted well before the legal track even began, showed that humans are very poor at making relevancy determinations in large data sets. This is a very inconvenient truth because it puts all precision and recall measurements in doubt. It means that the recall and precision measures we use are more like rough estimates than calculations. The measurements may be improved by expensive, remedial, three-pass expert human reviews and other methods, but even that has yet to be proven.[8]

This secret of human inadequacy and resulting measurement vagaries in large data-set reviews has been known in the information science world since at least 2000. I understand from Doug Oard, a well-known information scientist and one of the TREC Legal Track founders, that the problem of the "fuzziness" of relevance judgments remains an important and ongoing discussion among scientists. Apparently the fuzziness issue is far less of a problem when simply trying to compare one system with another (and determine which one is better) than it is when trying to report a correct

---

[8] *But see* Gordon V. Cormack & Maura R. Grossman, *Inconsistent Assessment of Responsiveness in E-Discovery: Difference of Opinion or Human Error?* DESI IV: The ICAIL 2011 Workshop on Setting Standards for Searching Electronically Stored Information in Discovery Proceedings (June 6, 2011) (humans can agree and create a gold standard if relevance is defined clearly enough to reviewers and if objective mistakes by reviewers, as opposed to subjective disagreements, are identified and corrected).

(absolute) value for some quantity, such as recall or precision. In my personal correspondence with Doug Oard on this issue, he advised:

> The Legal Track of TREC has generated quite a lot of attention to the problem of absolute evaluation simply because the law, properly, has a need for that information. But the law also has a need for relative evaluation (which can help to answer questions like "did you use the best available approach under the circumstances"), and "fuzziness" is well-known to have only limited effects on such relative comparisons.

Therefore, even though measurements may be too fuzzy to ever really say with any assurance that there is 95 to 99 percent accuracy, they can tell us how one method compares with another. For instance, we can know that keyword search is ineffective when compared with multimodal; we just cannot know exactly how well either of them do.

The fuzziness of recall measurements may explain the wide divergences in the measurements of search effectiveness. For instance, it could explain how the 2009 batch tests of keywords only measured a remarkably low 4 percent recall rate.[9] The rate may have been better than that—more in line with the usual 20 percent recall rates that other experiments have shown—but we do not really know because the gold standard measurements can fluctuate wildly. Again, this is all because the average one-pass human review is known to be unreliable.

William Webber

The fuzziness issue is one of several important topics addressed in an interesting paper written in 2011 by a young information scientist, William Webber, titled *Re-examining the Effectiveness of Manual Review.* Webber is an Australian now doing his postdoctoral work with Professor Oard. His paper arose out of an e-discovery search conference held in China. In his paper, Webber explained:

> It is well-known that human assessors frequently disagree on the relevance of a document to a topic. Voorhees [2000] found that experienced TREC assessors, albeit working from only

[9] *2009 TREC Legal Track Overview*, TREC legal track §3.10.9.

> sentence-length topic descriptions, had an average overlap (size of intersection divided by size of union) of between 40% and 50% on the documents they judged to be relevant. Voorhees concludes that 65% recall at 65% precision is the best retrieval effectiveness achievable, given the inherent uncertainty in human judgments of relevance. Bailey et al. [2008] survey other studies giving similar levels of inter-assessor agreement.[10]

Can anyone validly claim absolute recall or precision rates in large data-set reviews that are more than 65 percent when the determinations are made by single-pass human review? Apparently not—at least not in the experiments done at Trec up to 2010.

Webber's China paper goes on to explain the well-known study by Roitblat, Kershaw, and Oot[11]:

> For their study, the authors revisit the outcome of an earlier, in-house manual review. The original review surveyed a corpus of 2.3 million documents in response to a regulatory request, and produced 176,440 as responsive to the request; the process took four months and cost almost $14 million. Roitblat et al. had two automated systems and two manual review teams review the documents again for relevance to the original request.
>
> The automated systems worked on the entire corpus; the manual review teams looked at a sample of 5,000 documents. Roitblat et al. (Table 1) found that the overlap between the relevance sets of the two manual teams was only 28%, even lower than the 40% to 50% observed in Voorhees [2000] for TREC AdHoc assessors. The overlap between the new and the original productions was also low, 16% for each of the manual teams, and 21% and 23% for the automatic systems. …

---

[10] William Webber, *Re-examining the Effectiveness of Manual Review*, from the Special Interest Group on Information Retrieval (SIGIR) 2011 Information Retrieval for E-Discovery (SIRE) Workshop, July 28, 2011, Beijing, China.

[11] Roitblat, Kershaw & Oot, *Document Categorization in Legal Electronic Discovery: Computer Classification vs. Manual Review*, Journal of the American Society for Information Science and Technology, 61(1):70–80, 2010.

> The effectiveness scores calculated on the original production seemingly show that the automated systems are as reliable as the manual reviewers. However, as Roitblat et al. note, the original production is a questionable gold standard, since it likely is subject to the same variability in human assessment that the study itself demonstrates. Instead, the claim Roitblat et al. make for automated review is a more cautious one; namely, that two manual reviews are no more likely to produce results consistent with each other than an automated review is with either of them.
>
> Given the remarkably low level of agreement observed by Roitblat et al., their conclusion might seem a less than reassuring one; an attorney might ask not, which of these methods is superior, but, is either of these methods acceptable? More importantly, the study does not address the attorney's fundamental question: does automated or does manual review result in a production that more reliably meets the overseeing attorney's conception of relevance?[12]

Think about that: Lawyers are, on average, even worse than nonlawyers in making relevancy reviews. We only agree 28 percent of the time compared with earlier nonlawyer tests noted by Voorhees, which showed 40 percent agreement rates.[13] (In fairness, the studies by Voorhees were done with retired intelligence officers who were trained in document evaluation.) The 40 percent agreement rates showed that the best retrieval effectiveness achievable, given the inherent uncertainty in human judgments of relevance, was only 65 percent recall and 65 percent precision. What does the even lower 28 percent agreement rate found in the Roitblat et al. study mean? In private correspondence with Webber, he advised me that a 28 percent agreement rate produces a mean precision and recall rate of 44 percent.

To me, it seems as if Webber and Voorhees are saying that the best that lawyers can ever do using the gold standard of human review for measurement is something like 44 to 65 percent recall. Any measurements

---

[12] Webber, *supra.*

[13] Ellen M. Voorhees, *Variations in Relevance Judgments and the Measurement of Retrieval Effectiveness,* 36:5 INFORMATION PROCESSING & MANAGEMENT 697, 701 (2000).

higher than that are suspect because the gold standard itself is suspect. I think Webber, Voorhees, and others are saying that the human relevancy determinations lens we are using to study these processes is too fuzzy—too out of focus—to give us any real confidence in exactly what we are seeing; however, the fuzzy lens does allow us to compare one method against another.

The Triple-Pass Solution

Although I do not understand the math on the fuzziness issue, I understand it in an intuitive way from over 30 years of arguing with other attorneys and judges over relevancy, as well as from the thousands of vague requests for production I have read and tried to respond to. In the law, we use a kind of triple-pass quality-control method based on the disagreements of experts. The triple-pass method has evolved in the common law tradition over the past few centuries. We never simply rely on one tired lawyer's opinion. One lawyer expresses his or her view on relevance, then another lawyer (opposing counsel) uses his or her independent judgment to either agree or disagree (and, if they disagree, to object). A third expert, a judge, then hears arguments from both sides and makes a final determination. Without such triple-expert input and review, the determination of the relevance of evidence in legal proceedings would also be unreliable.

TREC has tried to use such a triple-pass method since 2009 to buttress the accuracy of its findings. The first reviewers make their determinations, then the participants make theirs. If the participants disagree, then the participants can ask for a ruling from the subject matter expert, who had been guiding the participants with up to 10 hours of consultation. The first review team has no such appeal rights and far less guidance. Also, the first-pass reviewers cannot present their side of the arguments to the judge. Not surprisingly under these conditions, if and when the participants appeal, the reports show that the expert judges usually rule with the participants. They have, after all, had ongoing ex parte communications with them and do not hear from the other side. This is not exactly the same triple play as in the real world of American justice, but it is far better than the flawed single-human review that Voorhees initially studied.

Not Too Fuzzy to Not Allow Valid Comparisons

Although the measures are fuzzy, they are not too fuzzy to not make comparisons between reviews. So, for instance, you can compare two human reviews and use the differences to show just how vague and inaccurate human review really is. This would be a comparison to establish the fuzziness of the gold standard you used to make recall, precision, and other measurements.

The study by Roitblat et al. sponsored by the Electronic Discovery Institute (EDI) did just that. It proved the incredible inconsistencies of single-pass human review in large data sets. This study examined a real-world event where Verizon paid $14,000,000 for contract reviewers to review 2.3 million documents in four months. (This is, by the way, a cost of $6.09 per document for review and logging only—a pretty good price for those days.) A second review by other reviewers commissioned by the study only agreed with 16 percent of the first determinations. Does that 16 percent agreement rate not suggest likely error rates of 84 percent?[14]

Surely, this study by EDI was the death blow to large-scale human reviews that are not in some way computer assisted to at least cull out documents before review. Why would anyone spend $14 million for such a poor-quality product after seeing this study? (I am told they still do this in the world of mergers and acquisitions and second reviews.) This is especially true when you consider that machine-assisted review is much faster and less expensive. Furthermore, as the studies also show, computer-assisted review is at least as reliable as most of the human reviewers (but maybe not all, as will be explained later).

With these limitations of human review and measurements in mind, consider the paper by Grossman and Cormack, which analyzed the 2009 TREC legal track studies on this issue:

> [T]he levels of performance achieved by two technology-assisted processes exceed those that would have been achieved by the official TREC assessors—law students and lawyers

---

[14] Roitblat et al., *supra*.

> employed by professional review companies—had they conducted a manual review of the entire document collection.[15]

This was good research and a great paper, but the gold standard was again just human reviewers and thus was subject to the vagaries of fuzzy measurement when it comes to calculating absolute values. As mentioned, TREC was working on this issue with their appeals process in 2010; however, due to economic constraints, it still differs from actual practice in several ways as mentioned. The first reviewers have relatively limited upfront instruction and training on the relevance issues, only limited contact with subject matter experts during the review, no testing or sampling feedback, and no appeal rights. Also, the human review in TREC 2009 did not meet the minimum ethical standards of supervision established by most state bar associations that have considered the propriety of delegated review to contract lawyers. Most bar associations require direct supervision of contract lawyers by counsel of record, which, in my opinion, requires direct and ongoing contact to supervise. Aside from the supervision issue, the statistics were skewed by a one-sided appeals process where the judge only heard one side of a relevancy argument from the party they trained in relevance. This reminds me of a secret for getting an *A* in law school from some professors: just tell them what you think they want to hear, not what you really think. For that reason, the win observed by Grossman and Cormack may not say as much about technology as it does about methodologies. Also, the paper focuses on the two technology-assisted processes that were better. What about the other technology-assisted processes that were not better?

Aside from these methodology concerns, as Webber pointed out, none of the studies up to 2010 by TREC or anyone else have addressed the key issue of concern to lawyers:

> ... which is not how much different review methods agreed or disagree with each other (as in the study by Roitblat et al. [2010]), nor even how close automated or manual review

---

[15]Maura R. Grossman & Gordon V. Cormack, *Technology-Assisted Review in e-Discovery Can Be More Effective and More Efficient than Exhaustive Manual Review*, 17:3 RICH. J. LAW TECH. 1–48 (2011) at 4.

methods turn out to have come to the topic authority's gold standard (as in the study by Grossman and Cormack [2011]). Rather, it is this: which method can a supervising attorney, actively involved in the process of production, most reliably employ to achieve their overriding goal, to create a production consistent with their conception of relevance.[16]

Hope for the Future

The TREC Legal Track was discontinued due to a series of issues—most of them political and having nothing to do with the funding and fuzziness issues discussed here. Although the problems noted with TREC have not been eliminated, they have been improved. A new track was started in 2015 that focused on the total recall issue.

I participated in the 2015 TREC as an individual lawyer using Kroll Ontrack software and the assistance of two of their experts, as did Catalyst. No other vendors joined us in the experiments, but maybe more will do so in 2016. The recall, precision, and F1 rates we attained were excellent—far higher than attained before. It vindicated multimodal search techniques using predictive coding. (The fuzziness issues still remain, but they have been mitigated.)

The 2015 TREC and the latest software and methodologies are subjects for another, more advanced book. For information on the latest results of current TREC research and more detailed explanations of the search methods I developed, see my websites: *www.MrEDR.com* and *www.AI-EnhancedReview.com.* A complete listing of the 60 or so articles I have written on legal search and predictive coding can also be found on my professional blog, *www.e-DiscoveryTeam.com.*

SUMMARIZING THE FIRST TWO SECRETS OF SEARCH

I can quickly summarize the first two secrets of search with popular slang: keyword search and manual review suck. Because most manual review is ineffective, most so-called objective measurements of precision and recall are unreliable. Keyword search would not perform quite so badly if it were not done blindly like a game of Go Fish, where it achieves

[16]Webber, *supra.*

really pathetic recall percentages in the 4 percent to 20 percent range (the TREC batch tasks). Keyword search, when tested and not merely guessed, still has an important place with smarter software and improved, cooperation-based multimodal search methods and quality controls. In that same vein, manual review can probably also be made good enough for accurate scientific measurements. However, in order to do so, the manual reviews would have to replicate the state-of-the-art methods we developed in private practice, which is expensive. We did this in the 2015 TREC research, with now-perfected hybrid multimodal methods and the latest versions of predictive coding software.[17]

Because the law already accepts linear manual review and keyword search as reasonable methods to respond to discovery requests, the law has set a very low standard. All you need to do to establish that an alternative method is legally reasonable is to show that it does as well as the previously accepted keyword and manual methods. This low hurdle was already cleared by the 2010 research, before the hiatus in TREC research. Therefore, we already have a green light under the law—or logically, we should have—to proceed with computer-assisted review. In fact, there are now more than 30 cases in the United States, Ireland, and the United Kingdom specifically approving and even encouraging the use of predictive coding. Conversely, no case has ever disallowed its use, although a few have refused to force litigants to use this method when they did not want to *and* they had already spent substantial sums on keyword, linear review.

If you want to dig deeper into the law of predictive coding, a quick Google search will lead you to many lists and discussions of this case law. This area of the law is widely publicized and grows every month. To help you get going in this research, start off with Judge Andrew Peck's two widely cited cases:

- *Da Silva Moore v. Publicis Group*, 287 F.R.D. 182 (S.D.N.Y., 2, 2012). This is the first case to approve predictive coding and is cited in most every case thereafter. The author was lucky to be involved in this case as the lead technology expert for the defense that requested the court's approval.

[17] *See, e.g., www.MrEDR.com.*

- *Rio Tinto PLC v. Vale S.A*, 306. F.R.D. 125 (S.N.D.Y. 2015). This is a kind of sequel to *Da Silva Moore*. In this opinion, Judge Peck cites the lead cases that have followed his 2012 breakthough opinion. Footnote 1 also discusses the issue of whether a party should be forced into using predictive coding if the request is made under the right circumstances, including before substantial sums have been spent using the old methods. Many believe that Judge Peck is prepared to enter such an order, as he has hinted as much at CLE events. Perhaps by the time of publication of this book, it will have already happened.

You could—and I think should—also conclude that any expectations that computer-assisted reviews have to be near perfect to be acceptable is misplaced. The claim that some vendors make about the near perfection of their search methods is counter to existing scientific research. It is wrong—mere marketing puff—because the manual-based measurements of recall and precision are too fuzzy to measure that closely. If any computer-assisted or other type of review comes up with 44 percent, it might in fact be perfect by an actual objective standard, and vice versa. Allegedly objective measurements of high recall rates in search are, at least before the 2015 TREC tests, an illusion. Moreover, this is a dangerous delusion because the misinformation could be used against producing parties to try to drive up the costs of production for ulterior motives.

In any event, most computer-assisted searches are already better than the average keyword or manual search, so it should be (and is) accepted as reasonable under the law without confidence inflation. We do not need perfection in the law, nor do we need to keep reviewing and re-reviewing to try to reach some magic, way-too-high measure of recall. We should always try to get as much of the truth as possible and should always try to improve. However, we should also remember that only so much truth can be afforded when we are faced with big data sets and limited financial resources. Proportionality is the pole star guiding all discovery, especially e-discovery.

As I have said time and again when discussing e-discovery efforts in general, including preservation-related efforts, the law demands reasonable efforts, not perfection. Now, science buttresses this position in document productions by showing that we have never had perfection in search of large numbers of documents—not with manual searches and certainly not with keyword searches.

THE THIRD SEARCH SECRET: RELEVANT IS IRRELEVANT

Relevant is irrelevant: This contradiction has more impact than the technically more accurate statement of "merely relevant documents in big data reviews are irrelevant as compared to highly relevant documents." In other words, all that counts in litigation are the hot documents—the highly relevant ones with strong probative value—not the documents that are just relevant or responsive. In fact, in big data collections, I could not care less about merely relevant documents. Their only purpose is to lead me to highly relevant documents. Moreover, as we will see in the fourth and final secret, I only care about a handful of those.

In a case involving tens of thousands, hundreds of thousands, or even millions of documents, almost all of the documents that are merely relevant will not be admissible into evidence. (I'll explain why in a minute.) For that reason alone, their discovery should be subject to very close scrutiny. The gathering of evidence for admission at trial is, after all, the only valid purpose of discovery. Discovery is never an end in itself, although many litigators (as opposed to true trial lawyers) and vendors often lose that track of that basic truth. Discovery is only permitted for purposes of preparation for trial. It is never permitted to extort one side into a settlement to avoid the costs of a document review or to at least gain a strategic edge, although we know that this happens all of the time.

Most merely relevant evidence will not be admissible for the same reason that most of the highly relevant evidence will not be admissible. Even though it is relevant, this evidence is a cumulative waste of time. For that reason, it is inadmissible under Rule 403 of the Federal Evidence Code (and its state law equivalents), which states the following:

> Rule 403. Excluding Relevant Evidence for Prejudice, Confusion, Waste of Time, or Other Reasons.
>
> The court may exclude relevant evidence if its probative value is substantially outweighed by a danger of one or more of the following: unfair prejudice, confusing the issues, misleading

> the jury, undue delay, wasting time, or needlessly presenting cumulative evidence.[18]

The typical fact scenario used in law school to exemplify the principle of cumulative evidence is a situation where 100 witnesses see the same accident. Each witness would give roughly the same description of the event and the testimony of each would be equally relevant. Still, the testimony of 100 witnesses would never be allowed because it would be a waste of time and/or a needless presentation of cumulative evidence to have all 100 witnesses repeat the same facts at trial. The same principle applies to documentary evidence. If there are 100 e-mails that show essentially the same relevant fact, you cannot admit all 100 of them. That would be a cumulative waste of time. The question of admissibility presented in Federal Rule of Evidence 403 requires a balancing of the costs and benefits of logically relevant evidence. This is sometimes referred to as the *Rule 403 balancing test*, which is similar to the proportionality balancing test in the 2015 revised Rule 26(b)(1) discussed previously.

The 2006 e-discovery Rule 26(b)(2)(B) has a similar balancing test for hard-to-access ESI, as does Rule 26(g), which requires only a reasonable inquiry of completeness in a response to discovery. Perhaps more importantly, Rule 26(g)(1)(B) also prohibits any request for discovery made "for any improper purpose, such as to harass, cause unnecessary delay, or needlessly increase the cost of litigation" and prohibits any request that is unreasonable or unduly burdensome or expensive "considering the needs of the case, prior discovery in the case, the amount in controversy, and the importance of the issues at stake in the action." All the rules point to proportional reasonability in discovery, a course of conduct not always followed in the past.[19]

The rules clearly state that cumulative evidence is not, or at least should not be, subject to discovery. It would be a disproportional waste of time and money. Thus, even though the documents might be

[18] *Also see* Rule 611. ("The court should exercise reasonable control over … presenting evidence so as to … (2) avoid wasting time.")

[19] *See* Patrick Oot, Anne Kershaw & Herbert L. Roitblat, *Mandating Reasonableness in a Reasonable Inquiry*, 87 DENVER U. LAW REV. 522–559 (2010), at 537–538.

relevant, if they are unreasonably cumulative, repetitive, or duplicative such that the burden outweighs the benefit, they are not only inadmissible as evidence, but they are, or should be, outside of discovery under revised Federal Rule of Civil Procedure 26(b)(1) (scope of discovery). This is buttressed by the prime directive of the Federal Rules of Civil Procedure, Rule 1.0. It requires all of the other rules of procedure to be interpreted and applied so as to make litigation just, speedy, and inexpensive. Again, recall how this key *rule of all rules* was strengthened by the 2015 amendments.

A survey that helped drive passage of the 2015 rule amendments shows how e-discovery spiraled out of control in many cases.[20] The 2010 survey was limited to large cases that went to trial in 2008. On average, 4,980,441 pages of documents were produced in discovery in these cases, but only 4,772 exhibit pages were entered into evidence.[21] That is a ratio of over 1,000 to 1! These are absurd numbers for a variety of reasons. The 4,772 pages admitted into evidence is ridiculous overkill, as will be shown further in the fourth secret, and so is the number of documents produced. The producing parties, acting in concert and cooperation with the requesting parties, should do a better job of culling down the irrelevant documents and marginally relevant documents. They are not needed for trial preparation.

The 2010 survey also offered an opinion convergent with my own that such discovery is excessive:

> Whatever marginal utility may exist in undertaking such broad discovery pales in light the costs.... Reform is clearly needed. A discovery system that requires the production of a field full

---

[20]Lawyers for Civil Justice et al., *Litigation Cost Survey of Major Companies* (2010), available at *http://www.uscourts.gov/file/document/institute-advancement-amer-legal-system-civil-litigation-survey*, App. 1 at 15 and Fig. 11.

[21]*Id* at pg. 3. *Also see DCG Sys., Inc. v. Checkpoint Techs., LLC*, No. C-11-03792 PSG, 2011 WL 5244356 (N.D. Cal. 2011) (little benefit to justify burden of large-scale e-mail production because on average only ".0074% of the documents produced actually made their way onto the trial exhibit list" and in appeals "email appears more rarely as relevant evidence").

of "haystacks" of information merely on the hope that the proverbial "needle" might exist and without any requirement for any showing that it actually does exist, creates a suffocating burden on the producing party. Despite this, courts almost never allocate costs to equalize the burden of discovery.[22]

THE FOURTH SECRET OF SEARCH: 7±2 SHOULD CONTROL ALL E-DISCOVERY

We have already established that the purpose of discovery is to prepare for trial. However, we have to understand the purpose of a trial to be able to grasp the fourth secret: 7±2. The purpose of all trials is to persuade. It is a level playing field where lawyers try to persuade a judge and/or jury as to what happened and what should be done about it. In this place of trial of humans by humans, the rule of 7±2 reigns supreme. It always has and, unless we allow robots as jurors, always will. Unfortunately, most litigators are unaware of this rule of the transmission of information—or if they do know of it, most fail to see its connection to discovery and search. The rule of 7±2 now has little place in e-discovery analysis.

This rule is a secret; because it is unknown, we have gone astray in e-discovery. Vast sums of money are routinely wasted in the production of fields full of "haystacks" of information. Because the secret has not yet been heard and its clear implications have not yet been understood, trial lawyers everywhere still scratch their heads in disbelief at the sheer mention of e-discovery.

I hesitate to go to this deep place of information transmission and cognitive limitations; however, to keep the search for truth and justice on track, I really have no choice. We must, like the Pythagoreans of old, consider the significance of the number 7 and its impact on our work, especially on our conceptions of proportionality.

The fourth secret of search is based on the legal art of persuasion and the limitations of information transmission. No jury member can

[22]Lawyers for Civil Justice et al., *supra*. Statement found in original survey located at *http://www.uscourts.gov/file/document/litigation-cost-survey-major-companies* but deleted in subsequent drafts.

possibly hold more than five to nine documents in his or her head at a time. It is a waste of time to build a jury case around more documents than that. Judges who are trained in the law and are quite comfortable with documents can do a little better, but not that much. In a bench trial, you might be able to use eight to twelve documents to persuade the skilled judge. But even then, you may be pushing your luck. Judges, after all, have a lot on their minds, and your particular case is just one among hundreds (or in state court, thousands).

Computers Expand Document Counts, Not Minds

Even though the computerization of society has exploded the number of documents we retain by a trillion-fold, the ability of the human mind to remember and process has remained the same. We still can only be persuaded by a handful of writings, as that is all of the information we can retain. Presenting dozens of documents is a waste of time. The only reason to present more than five to nine documents at trial is to provide context and an evidentiary foundation. The few dozen other documents that you may need at trial are merely window dressing, a frame for the real art.

A computer can easily process and recall millions of documents in minutes, but we cannot. Even fast readers are limited to reading about 500 words per minute or a skim-review rate of 1,000 words per minute. No matter how much time we may have (and in legal proceedings, time is always constrained), our ability to read, understand, and comprehend relevant writings is limited. This is especially true in the high pressure and expedited schedule of a trial and formal presentation of evidence in court. Therefore, experienced trial lawyers may agree that the average juror is likely to remember and be influenced by only a handful of documents. (By the way, this rule of seven in persuasion is a corollary to the KISS principle ["Keep it simple, stupid"], well known to all persuaders, along with "Tell-tell-and-tell.")

Although most trial lawyers learn this guideline from hard experience, there is good theoretical support in psychology for such memory limitations. It is sometimes called Miller's law, after cognitive psychologist George A. Miller, a professor at Princeton University. Professor Miller first described this limitation of human cognition in a 1956 article that may be the most widely quoted psychology paper of all time.[23] Miller's paper suggests that seven (plus or minus two) is the magic number that characterizes people's memory performance on random lists of letters, words, numbers, or almost any kind of meaningful familiar item. He essentially found that human beings were only capable of receiving, processing, and remembering seven (plus or minus two) variables at any one time. Miller ends his famous paper on the limits of our capacity to process information with this somewhat odd remark, especially considering his reputation as a scientist:

> What about the magical number seven? What about the seven wonders of the world, the seven seas, the seven deadly sins, the seven daughters of Atlas in the Pleiades, the seven ages of man, the seven levels of hell, the seven primary colors, the seven notes of the musical scale, and the seven days of the week? What about the seven-point rating scale, the seven categories for absolute judgment, the seven objects in the span of attention, and the seven digits in the span of immediate memory? For the present I propose to withhold judgment. Perhaps there is something deep and profound behind all these sevens, something just calling out for us to discover it. But I suspect that it is only a pernicious, Pythagorean coincidence.[24]

Some psychologists think that Miller overestimated the average human capacity when he said it was between five and nine. They think the limit is more likely to be from two to six, with the magic number being four, not seven.[25] In any event, it is not hundreds of documents, much less thousands or millions. Yet in an average large case today, 4,980,441 pages of documents are produced and 4,772 pages are allowed into evidence. What is wrong with this picture? The discovery chase has lost track of the goal. An experienced trial lawyer, who may use

---

[23]George A. Miller, *The Magical Number Seven, Plus or Minus Two: Some Limits on Our Capacity for Processing Information*, 63 PSYCH. REV. 81–97.

[24]*Id*, at 42–43.

[25]Jeanne Farrington, *Seven Plus or Minus Two*, 23 PERFORMANCE IMPROVEMENT QUARTERLY 113–116 (2011).

hundreds of exhibits in a very large trial for context and technical reasons, will still only focus on five to nine documents. He or she knows that jurors cannot handle more information than that. The rest of the documents that go into evidence will have little or no real persuasive value.

The limitations of the human mind thus provide a consistency and continuity with the trials and systems of justice of our past pre-computer civilizations. No matter how many more documents may exist today within the technical scope of legal relevance, our jurors' capacities are the same. The art of legal persuasion remains the same. These mental persuasion limits govern the number of documents useful to a trial lawyer, judge, and jury. The human mind has its limits. Computer discovery must start to realize these limits and take them into consideration. This is a basic truth that e-discoverers have lost sight of. It is the core of why most old-time trial lawyers think the whole business of e-discovery is ridiculous. It is high time for the secret of seven to be outed and, more importantly, to be followed. The rule of seven should have significant consequences on our legal practice and scientific research.

Uneducated Searchers Will Never Find the Top 7±2

The location of the few highly relevant documents has always been a problem in the law. However, in the low-volume paper world, it was never an overwhelming one. The paper document search-and-retrieval process was a relatively simple problem traditionally assigned to the youngest, most inexperienced lawyers. Today, the search for the smoking e-guns is much more difficult than ever before, yet untrained young associates are still commonly given this task. Many are simply told to go do e-discovery. They are provided with little more training than attendance of a few CLEs, which, as you may know, may not teach you that much. That is one compelling reason I took the time to make my law school training program available online to attorneys, paralegals, techs, and students everywhere (*www.E-DiscoveryTeam-Training.com*). It provides more than 75 hours of instruction, which is what it takes to really learn something. Just don't try to learn more than seven things at a time. Take your time and study online whenever it is convenient to you.

Lack of real education is the primary impediment to further progress in all e-discovery issues, including search. Patrick Oot, Anne Kershaw, and Herbert Roitblat explained it well in their excellent *Mandating Reasonableness* article:

> The problem is not technology; it is attorneys' lack of education and the judicial system's inattentiveness to ensure that attorneys have the proper education and training necessary for a proportional and efficient discovery process. Lack of attorney education aggravates the problem because uneducated litigators are unable to make informed judgments as to where to draw the line on discovery, thereby creating unrealistic expectations from the courts—particularly as to costs and burdens. For example, failing to understand how different methods of search methodology work, some judges will unnecessarily mandate traditional and expensive "brute force" attorney review.... Simply put, the legal system has a crisis of education. Both attorneys and judges need to better understand technology as it applies to the reasonable inquiry.[26]

Just Give Me the Smoking Guns

Because only a few documents are needed for analysis of a case and even less for persuasion at trial, paper-only search has sufficed until recently for most trial lawyers. Lawyers found the few documents they needed in printouts. However, those days are now all but gone. The few important documents found by paper searches, and even by ESI searches that are driven by old paper-based systems, are not likely to uncover the best documents. The smoking guns will remain hidden in the data deluge. Lawyers will not find the top seven needed for the judge and jury.

As the nature of documents changes and the previously noted habits of witnesses to print key documents disappears, this problem will worsen. No one today says incriminating things in paper letters. Very few still even write paper letters. They say it in e-mails, text messages,

[26]Oot et al., *Mandating Reasonableness, supra* at 545, 547.

instant messages, Facebook posts, blogs, tweets, etc.—and almost no one prints these and puts them in filing cabinets.

There is a key lesson for e-discovery in the trial lawyer wisdom of seven. To be useful, discovery must drastically cull the millions of ESI files that may be relevant down to the few hundred that are useful, then to the five or nine really needed for persuasion. Culling down from millions to only tens of thousands is not serving the needs of the law. It is a pointless waste of resources and a waste of client money. A production of tens of thousands of documents, not to mention hundreds of thousands, is unjust, slow, and inefficient.

Many vendors today brag about how their smart culling was able to eliminate up to 80 percent of the corpus. They will tell you this is an excellent cull rate before you begin review. It is not. They may also tell you that it is unreasonable for you to try to cull out more than that. They are wrong. They have a financial motivation to take such conservative positions. The more documents you review, the more money they make. Some law firms see it that way, too. However, they won't last. The firm's clients will eventually catch on and switch their work away from the haystack builders.

Even if well intentioned, many vendors (and lawyers) do not understand that the law requires only reasonable efforts and proportional efforts, not perfect or exhaustive efforts. (This failure of understanding was part of the 2015 rule amendments.) Many lawyers and vendors do not understand the basic limitations of a trial or cumulative evidence. Many have never even seen a trial, much less tried one.

Vendors are not supposed to give legal advice, yet I hear them do it all of the time when, for instance, they talk about how much you should review to meet your obligations under the law. They may say it would be very risky to try to cull out too many documents—as if they could ever really eliminate risk, much less quantify risk. The only way to eliminate risk is by cooperation or court order, not by following a vendor's best practice suggestions.

When you understand the third and fourth search secrets, you realize that a cull rate of at least 90 percent is proportional. It does not matter if you weed out a few merely relevant documents. If you have a million files, you should be able to weed out at least 90 percent (900,000 documents) before you begin review. In fact, you should aim for elimination of at least 98 percent by using relevancy ranking; only do a human hybrid review of the remaining 20,000 documents.

New e-discovery search and culling methods need to be perfected to limit the quantity of documents to a size that the human mind can deal with and comprehend. The processes should try to find all, or nearly all, of the highly relevant documents, even if a significant percentage of marginally relevant documents are missed. Who cares about these technically relevant documents? No one, except maybe those dazzled by recall statistics who do not understand the natural speed limits of the mind, nor the revised rules of discovery. All that really matters are the hot documents. That is the lesson of the third secret of search—that relevant is irrelevant.

The lesson of the fourth secret, 7±2, is that the true goal of e-discovery should be the five to nine of the hot documents that the triers of fact can understand. If your search finds those magic seven and no others, it is a great success, regardless of all of its other misses. If your search finds a million relevant documents, attains a precision and recall rate of 99 percent, but misses the top seven key documents, it is a complete failure. We have to change our search methods to focus on the top seven.

Change the Scientific Testing

We also have to redesign our scientific testing to measure what really counts, the 7±2, plus time and money. I suggest that TREC have tests involving a *seeded* test set where all searchers look to find seven planted "Easter eggs." Whoever finds them all (or finds the most), and does so the fastest and at the least expense, gets the highest score. In fact, for the tests to be fair and realistic, they should be time limited and cost limited. Participants should no longer be allowed to keep that secret. (This last reform was accepted by TREC in the 2015 Recall Track.) In the law, time and money matter. A search process is worthless if it costs too much or takes too long.

So far, all of the scientific experiments I have heard about in e-discovery have measured effectiveness (meaning how well or poorly a search performs) by only looking at relevance measures, primarily precision and recall (or the harmonic mean thereof, F1). However, in information science, relevance is just one of the four basic measures of search effectiveness. The other three are efficiency, utility, and user satisfaction. According to Dominich, the efficiency measures are the costs of search and the time it takes.[27] We need to start to include efficiency measures in our tests, as well as provide heavy ranking to our relevance measures.

In Law, One Key Document Is Worth a Million Relevant Documents

Too few experts in e-discovery today understand the fourth secret of search—namely the magic limiting power of seven. On the other hand, all experienced trial lawyers seem to know it well, even if they have never heard of Professor Miller. As a result of 7±2 being such a secret to many of my friends in e-discovery, they have erroneously focused on an effort to recall as many relevant documents as possible. They pride themselves in amassing large volumes of relevant documents, when in fact that is the last thing real trial lawyers want. They do not want 10,000 relevant documents; they want 10. They want just a handful of killer documents that will help persuade the jury by making their story clear and convincing. The failure of e-discovery proponents to focus on this is another reason that many lawyers think that e-discovery is stupid.

Electronic discovery search is not an academic game to be played. It is all about finding evidence for trial. Statistics and methods are worthless unless they properly weigh recall statistics by persuasive impact. One highly relevant document can—and usually does—counteract 10 million relevant ones. It is like one grandmaster at chess playing a thousand amateurs. The amateurs do not have a chance. Because of this, if your search is not designed to find the five to nine most persuasive documents, then your search is flawed—no matter what your precision and recall rates are. High recall rates are only imperative for highly relevant documents, the hot documents. Nothing else matters, except for the costs involved—the time and money it takes to find evidence. If you don't focus your search on the 7±2 hottest documents, you may never find them.

---

[27] Sándor Dominich, *The Modern Algebra of Information* (Springer-Verlag 2008) at 87–88.

Some believe that you have to find all of the relevant documents in order to be able to find the top 7±2. That was true in the paper world of linear review of hundreds of documents, but it is not true in large-scale electronic review. You can now use software that focuses its search on the highly ranked relevant documents. However, you have to adopt your methods accordingly.

New methods for ESI review that focus on the retrieval of ranked relevancy, not just relevancy, should be used. The methods should focus on finding the hot documents with the understanding that merely responsive documents are, due to their extreme number, of little importance. Relevant is irrelevant. The same ranking applies to the identification of privileged and confidential ESI. If one hot privileged document is missed in a privilege review, it can be far more damaging than the inadvertent production of hundreds of marginally privileged ones.

The bottom line is this: To follow the third and fourth secrets, the key feature you should look for in search software is the ability to accurately rank the probable relevant documents. Ranking must be a far more sophisticated function than simply counting the number of times a keyword or pattern appears in a document. It should epitomize all of the criteria and indices used by the software black box—latent semantic, four-dimensional geometric, or otherwise.

The ideal e-discovery Watson computer must not only search and find—it must rank, with the highest on top. Watson may not be able to put the five documents you will use as the first five documents in the ranked list, but it is not too much to expect that the 7±2 will be in the top 5,000. The humans working with Watson will narrow them down, and the trial lawyers making the pitch at trial will make the final selections.

RECAP OF ALL FOUR SECRETS

The first secret discussed in this chapter is that *keyword search sucks.* Most attorneys still using this old method are searching for ESI the wrong way. One qualification to that secret is that keyword search does not perform badly if it is used with other search methods in a tested multimodal process.

The second secret is that large-scale linear manual reviews are also ineffective. This throws into question all human-only based "gold standards" by which to make precision and recall measurements.

The third secret is that *relevant is irrelevant*—smart culling that follows best practices is required by the rules to keep the time and cost of review proportional.

The fourth secret was gleaned from psychologists and trial lawyers: 7±2. It reminds us of the true goal of e-discovery and the need to heavily weight and constrain our relevancy searches.

As you have no doubt guessed by now, my real goal here was not to give away secrets, but to lay the foundation for new standards of search and review. My work on this continues, but it is too complex for inclusion in this book. Interested readers who want to dig deeper into legal search are referred to my professional blog, *www.e-DiscoveryTeam.com,* and the links within to many articles on document review and predictive coding. You may also see *www.LegalSearchScience.com*, which is one of several free educational websites that I have devoted to this topic.

CONCLUSION

Way back in 1947, the Supreme Court in *Hickman v. Taylor*, the landmark case on discovery, stated that "[m]utual knowledge of all the relevant facts gathered by both parties is essential to proper litigation."[28] The opinion was written by Justice Frank Murphy (1890–1949). Today, his statement is obsolete because it says that *all* of the relevant facts gathered should be shared. This statement was reasonable when written in 1947, but not today. In those days, all of the relevant facts could be found in a few dozen documents. In the 1960s, that became at most a few hundred. In the 1970s and 1980s, that number increased to a few thousand. Today, we live in a completely different world. Written words profligate and multiply with the help of computers in a way that our ancestors could never have imagined. Now, you can gather hundreds of thousands or millions of relevant documents in even small cases. We write all of the time, and so do our machines; our writings multiply and remain, albeit in electronic form only.

---

[28] 329 U.S. 495, 507 (1947).

The sharing of marginally important knowledge is no longer essential to proper litigation. In fact, as we have seen, it is contrary to the rules, especially Rule 26 of the Federal Rules of Civil Procedure. Most merely relevant documents today are inadmissible.[29] They are a cumulative waste of time. It is unreasonable to gather them, much less disclose them. Rule 1.0 prohibits such a waste of time and money. Moreover, it is unjust, for it is easy to bury the truth in mountains of technically relevant haystacks. Document dumps are a way to hide the truth that is essential to proper litigation.

We need to design our e-discovery to be reasonably calculated to lead to admissible, noncumulative evidence. We need to focus on the hot documents. We need to remember that all that really matters are the five to nine hottest documents. This is what the trial lawyers need to tell their story of prosecution or defense. The few other documents that you may want to put into evidence are just window dressing. The millions of other technically relevant documents are of little or no use in the preparation for trial—and of no use whatsoever in the conduct of a trial.

Therefore, we need smart AI-enhanced software tools, which we can teach to find the hottest documents. This software should have ranking built in as a core function. It also means that we need informed e-discovery attorneys who understand the secrets of search. They can then bridge the gap that now exists with trial lawyers. Perhaps then, the current e-discovery strategy of avoidance used by many lawyers today will be abandoned. Then, maybe all lawyers will adopt proportional e-discovery designed for trial.

---

[29]Rule 403, *Federal Rules of Evidence.*

9 On Common Sense and Litigation Holds

To me (and most others who look at this issue), it is just common sense to send out a written litigation hold notice, not simply provide oral notice. The Chief Judge for the United States District Court in Idaho, Judge B. Lynn Winmill, certainly agrees:

> Generally not deleting documents, and orally requesting certain employees to preserve relevant documents concurrently with filing a lawsuit, is completely inadequate. It is very risky—to such an extent that it borders on recklessness.[1]

This opinion is filled with many excellent observations, comments, and rulings on the important issues surrounding litigation holds.

VERBAL HOLD NOTICE CONTROVERSY

The verbal hold controversy, like so many others in e-discovery law, was started by Judge Scheindlin. In her landmark *Pension Committee* opinion, she held that it was gross negligence not to do several things to implement a litigation hold—one of which was to send out a hold notice

[1]Scentsy Inc. v. B.R. Chase LLC, No. 1:11-cv-00249-BLW, 2012 WL 4523112 at *8 (D. Idaho Oct. 2, 2012).

in writing and not rely on verbal notice alone.[2] On this verbal versus writing issue, it seems to me that Judge Scheindlin was clearly right. Let us accept this as a bright line and move on to the other preservation issues raised in *Pension Committee.* After all, everyone seems to agree that the whole area of preservation law needs more certainty. (That was one of the strongest arguments for a complete rewrite of Rule 37(e) in the 2015 amendments.)

Let us argue instead about the consequences of failure to provide written notice. That is a more productive analysis instead of focusing on whether crossing the line on no notice is gross or simple negligence and the consequences of this omission. (That is what the 2015 revised Rule 37(e) purports to do—make it clear that negligence and gross negligence alone are insufficient for the imposition of case dispositive sanctions.) Lawyers should do everything in their power to be sure that litigants send out *written* hold notices. This is not a pro-plaintiff issue, as the *Scentsy* case demonstrates, because the negligent notifier was the plaintiff. It is a pro-evidence issue. I am in favor of requiring reasonable, proportionate efforts (not perfect efforts) to preserve evidence, and it is certainly reasonable to require that a notice be in writing. It is what I would call a *standard practice* for any size suit—the bare minimum to avoid negligence. The content and other details of written notice, and the other actions you take to preserve b*eyond just generally not deleting documents,* crosses over into the higher realms of better and best practices.

A written notice has long been a part of any e-discovery attorney's minimum acceptable standards when it comes to preservation. It is so easy to do. You can tell people to preserve in person or by phone, but also send out an e-mail to confirm the notice. I do acknowledge one exception (and I feel sure that Judge Scheindlin and Judge Winmill would both agree)—a situation with a one-person company. Sending a written hold notice to yourself does seem more silly than reasonable. However, even then, a memorandum of all preservation activities taken by the one-person company to preserve would be in order.

---

[2] Committee of the University of Montreal Pension Plan v. Banc of America Securities, LLC, 685 F. Supp. 2d 456, 465 (S.D.N.Y. 2010).

When you have a situation with multiple employees that might have evidence, even in a small company, I have never heard any expert *recommend* reliance on oral hold notices alone. It is usually a losing argument to attack this point in *Pension Committee,* as *Scentsy* shows. Argue about the other litigation hold requirements set forth in *Pension Committee* if you will—remedies, the blind *per se* classifications, causation, or severity of sanctions—but not about requiring the hold notice to be in writing.[3]

Because a few experts, including judges, disagree with me on this and would prefer to avoid all bright lines when it comes to preservation notices, it was gratifying to see that Judge Winmill agrees with my position on *Scentsy.*[4]

THERE IS FAR MORE TO PRESERVATION THAN THE BARE MINIMUM OF NOTICE

Scentsy not only examines the oral hold notice issue, but also the issue of when a duty to preserve is triggered. Certainly, the duty for a plaintiff will always be triggered before a suit is filed, so there will always be a pre-litigation duty to preserve. The duty of a defendant may also

---

[3] *See, e.g.,* Surowiec v. Capital Title Agency, 790 F. Supp. 2d 997, 1007 (D. Ariz. 2011) (rejecting *Pension Committee*'s holding that failure to issue a litigation hold constitutes "gross negligence per se" because "[p]er se rules are too inflexible for this factually complex arc of the law"); Deyo, *Deconstructing Pension Committee: The Evolving Rules of Evidence Spoliation and Sanctions in the Electronic Discovery Era,* 75 ALB. L. REV. 305 (2011/2012); Port Authority Police Asian Jade Soc. of N.Y. & N.J. v. Port Auth. of N.Y. & N.J., 601 F. Supp. 2d 566, 569 (S.D.N.Y. 2009) *affirmed* Chin v. The Port Authority, 685 F.3d 135 (2d Cir. 2012) ("We reject the notion that a failure to institute a 'litigation hold' constitutes gross negligence per se. Rather, we agree that 'the better approach is to consider [the failure to adopt good preservation practices] as one factor' in the determination of whether discovery sanctions should issue."); Maese, Barnett & Stelcen, *Second Circuit Rejects Bright-Line Test for Failure to Issue Hold Notice*, N.Y. LAW J (2012).

[4] *But see* Orbit One Communications, Inc. v. Numerex Corp., 2010 WL 4615547 (S.D.N.Y. Oct. 26, 2010) (J. Francis); Merck Eprova AG v. Gnosis S.P.A., 2010 WL 1631519, at *4 (S.D.N.Y. Apr. 20, 2010) (J. Sullivan).

sometimes be triggered before suit, but that depends on a number of factors.

The issues of hold timing, notice contents, notice recipients, and other actions that should be taken in a particular case to preserve evidence are issues present in every case. These are legal activities requiring skilled legal judgment. That is why I created, with the help of a few friends, the Electronic Discovery Best Practices site (*www.EDBP.com*). It is devoted to three out of the 10 attorney on preservation related activities, as represented by the second column squares in the electronic discovery best practices (EDBP) workflow chart practices (Hold Notices, Interviews, and Collections).

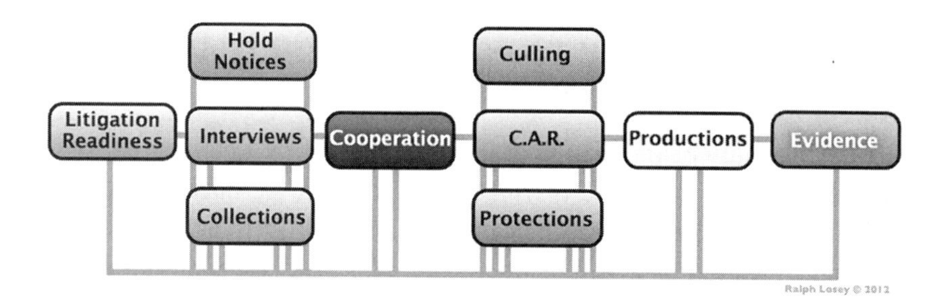

All novices to e-discovery should study these sections of EDBP carefully. After all, every case has ESI preservation issues—unless, of course, you represent a client that has no computers. (Do any such clients still exist?)

MAKING GOOD SENSE WITHOUT SCHEINDLIN

Scentsy is a copyright and trade dress infringement case in the high-stakes industry of scented candles. The name of the lead primary defendant is Harmony. You would think maybe they could settle their disputes over a good cup of tea and a few *Oms*, but no. The companies sued each other instead, then got into a number of expensive discovery disputes.[5]

The first part of the opinion addresses some of the non-e-discovery disputes that had been resolved by the magistrate and were appealed,

[5]Scentsy Inc. v. B.R. Chase LLC, No. 1:11-cv-00249-BLW, 2012 WL 4523112 (D. Idaho 2012).

including an interesting argument over attorney-eyes-only confidentiality. The last third of the opinion concerns the e-discovery preservation dispute, which arises out of the *Defendants' Motion to Compel Forensic Examination and/or Other Appropriate Relief.*[6] That is where the preservation and verbal hold notice issues are discussed.

First, it is very interesting to note that although *Scentsy* reads like Schiendlin in *Pension Committee*, neither her name, nor any of her cases (including *Pension Committee*) are ever mentioned. How could this dispute be briefed without either side mentioning *Pension Committee*?

To my mind, this makes Judge Winmill's holding all the more important. Even if you hide *Pension Committee* from your local judge (and after all, it was not binding authority, just another district court opinion from outside of your circuit, which would not have to be cited), your judge is likely to reach the same opinion. It is just good common sense.

JUDGE WINMILL TELLS THE "SCENTILLATING" STORY

As in so many cases, the devil is in the details, and they are set forth clearly and concisely in *Scentsy*. Judge Lynn Winmill is a good writer who sniffs out the truth from the competing arguments. Judge Winmill is a 1977 Harvard Law graduate who has been a judge since 1987, and a district court judge since 1995. Here are Judge Winmill's own words candling out the maliferous mess of the plaintiff's preservation failures (for ease of reading, I have deleted Judge Winmill's many citations to the record):

> Here, Scentsy, the plaintiff, did not issue a written litigation hold to anyone at Scentsy. Instead, its General Counsel, Eric Ritter, "spoke to the individuals that would have information regarding Harmony Homes or the subject warmers, and asked—requested that those documents not be deleted...." There is some dispute about when Scentsy first anticipated litigation in this matter, with Harmony suggesting it was May 2010, and Scentsy suggesting it was March 2011. The lawsuit

[6] *Id.* at *6.

> was filed in May 2011. Ritter issued his oral litigation hold "roughly concurrent with the filing of the Complaint." Scentsy's document retention policy routinely deletes emails, but not other documents, that are over six months old.[7]

Other parts of the opinion explain that any user can delete any of their documents at any time, including their e-mail and attachments, at their own discretion and judgment. One custodian could keep all of their documents forever, whereas another could delete right away. The e-mail system has an automated deletion system in place where all e-mail and attachments are deleted after six months. (The opinion does not say if custodians can circumvent that by creating their own personal archives as PST files, but I strongly suspect they can.) Aside from e-mail, no other Scentsy document repository had an autodelete function in place.

Scentsy's failure to create a consistent document retention policy, including e-mail, was an error that set up this spoliation attack. Judges tend to react adversely to a complete *laissez-faire*, do whatever you want, type of nonpolicy. Many users like that kind of freedom, but it creates additional organizational risk when faced with litigation. That is one reason why most experts today recommend consistent ESI retention policies as a best practice. The policies must be closely integrated with litigation hold policies and procedures. This is a critical part of pre-suit litigation readiness, which is the first step in the 10-step attorney-centric EDBP. All e-discovery lawyers should be familiar with litigation readiness best practices and try to help their clients to implement them.

Now back to the *Scentsy* story in Winmill's words:

> Harmony suggests that Scentsy has failed to produce key documents because of an insufficient litigation hold. Essentially, Harmony accuses Scentsy of spoliation. Spoliation occurs when a party destroys or alters evidence, or fails to preserve evidence for another party in pending or reasonably foreseeable litigation. Harmony asks the Court to compel Scentsy to conduct a forensic exam of its own computer systems at its own

[7] *Id.* at *7.

> expense to retrieve any deleted discoverable data, or to order other appropriate sanctions.[8]

It was easy for defendants here to prove that Scentsy had destroyed evidence after a hold was instituted. If nothing else, e-mail was automatically destroyed after it hit its six-month trigger for auto-delete. The only real problem that the defendants had for a spoliation claim was to show that any of the e-mail deleted was actually ESI relevant to this lawsuit. The defendants cleverly did not seek overkill as punishment for the spoliation. They did not seek case-ending sanctions or an adverse inference instruction. Instead, they sought very expensive studies, forensic examinations, of Scentsy's computers. Those examinations might show relevant evidence had been destroyed, or they might not. However, it was a win-win for the defendants because of the enormous burden the costs of the exercise would place on the plaintiff. The plaintiff might be forced to accept a low-ball settlement offer rather than pay for the forensic examinations. Yes, there is a lot of strategy and posturing going on here. I think that Judge Winmill understood all of that perfectly well, as you will see in a minute by his remedy. But first, he sniffs out more of the key facts of Scentsy's cascading errors:

> The Court has serious concerns with Scentsy's retention policy and litigation hold process. Generally not deleting documents, and orally requesting certain employees to preserve relevant documents concurrently with filing a lawsuit, is completely inadequate. It is very risky—to such an extent that it borders on recklessness. However, in this case there is very little chance that any of the documents at issue in the pending motion were destroyed because of the policy. The Court has been provided with no reason to question Scentsy's representation that the bulk of the documents were inadvertently destroyed when Stewart's hard drive crashed, and that this occurred before Scentsy even knew about Harmony. Scentsy has provided the Court with testimony, given under oath, to that effect. Harmony has provided no evidence to the contrary.[9]

---

[8] *Id.* at *6.
[9] *Id.* at *8.

Note that Judge Winmill dislikes both Scentsy's ad-hoc retention policies and its loose and ineffective litigation hold policies. However, the defendants could offer no evidence that Scentsy's negligence, even though it was gross and bordered on recklessness, actually caused any damage. Instead, the evidence seemed to suggest that the only critical evidence lost was caused by an accidental hard-drive crash—no proximate causation. Still, Judge Winmill did not like what he had seen here and wanted to leave the door open for the defendant to sniff around some more for any indications of bad faith by Scentsy.

> However, there is a chance that some documents— particularly those related to the three warmers designed by someone other than Stewart—were destroyed after Scentsy anticipated this litigation. Scentsy's Vice President of Information Technology states that "[a]ll non e-mail documents saved to an employee's personal computer hard drive or to the Scentsy server are preserved indefinitely." However, Scentsy's General Counsel, Eric Ritter, suggests there really is no retention policy for such documents. He does state that "[f]iles other than emails are stored in accordance with the file creator's intent. In other words, we don't delete data off of user drives." Same goes for an Illustrator or Adobe file on a shared drive. But he further states that if anybody at Scentsy created a Word document on their user drive, it "would remain there until [he or she] removed it from the user drive." The same is true for the Illustrator and Adobe files on a shared drive. Illustrator documents, which were typically used to design the warmers, were kept on personal computers or the Scentsy Server.[10]

This quote shows how ad-hoc, every-person-for-themselves type retention policies and practices can come back to bite you when litigation erupts. The danger from these nonexistent policies was compounded tenfold by the failure to implement a proper litigation hold in a timely manner.

[10] *Id.* at *8.

> Ritter did not issue his oral litigation hold until "roughly concurrent with the filing of the Complaint." Thus, even if the Court accepts Scentsy's argument that it did not anticipate litigation until March 2011, there is at least a two-month window where these documents could have been destroyed by a user after Scentsy anticipated litigation if they were saved on a user computer or the server. If you accept Harmony's contention that Scentsy anticipated litigation as early as May of 2010, the window grows to 12 months. Regardless of which you accept, the Court recognizes that the likelihood that this occurred is slight. However, there is no way to know, and that uncertainty was caused by Scentsy's inadequate retention policy coupled with its late and imprecise litigation hold.[11]

Again, the one-two punch is at work to harm Scentsy here: an inadequate retention policy and imprecise litigation hold. Scentsy could have avoided both of these problems and have been in a better position to prevail in this litigation had it employed best practices in litigation readiness to tighten up these policies and protocols.

PROPORTIONAL REMEDY

Now we come to the all-important remedy part of the opinion. Here, note Judge Winmill's wise application of the proportionality doctrine way before the 2015 rules amendment. As is often the case, he applies the doctrine without ever using the term *proportionality,* but by citing a secondary (pre-2015 amendments) proportionality Rule 26(b)(2)(B), which in turn cited to the primary proportionality Rule 26(b)(2)(C).

> The remedy for Scentsy's inadequate policies is not simple to craft. Scentsy explains that, based upon a quote from an outside vendor, completing a forensic examination of its computer system would be lengthy and costly—even into the millions of dollars. Harmony does not dispute this. Thus, ordering the forensic exam under these circumstances would be an undue burden and cost. Fed.R.Civ.P. 26(b)(2)(B).

---

[11] *Id.* at *8.

However, Scentsy should not be completely let off the hook simply because the cost is high. As explained above, the Court has inherent power to make evidentiary rulings in response to the destruction of relevant evidence if spoliation occurs before the litigation is filed. *Unigard Security Insurance Co. v. Lakewood*, 982 F.2d 363 (9th Cir.1992). Under these circumstances, the Court will allow Harmony to depose the appropriate individuals—whether it be the individuals who designed the three warmers not designed by Stewart, or someone else at Scentsy—to determine whether anyone destroyed relevant documents regarding those warmers. The deposition costs, including Harmony's attorney fees for taking the depositions, shall be paid by Scentsy. If information is uncovered that spoliation occurred, the Court will consider giving an adverse inference instruction at trial or dismissing some or all of Scentsy's claims. Spoliation is a serious matter, and Scentsy's document retention and litigation hold policies are clearly unacceptable. The Court assumes that Scentsy will improve those policies in any future litigation. The failure to do so may result in this or some other court finding that Scentsy's failure to act, in the face of the warnings given in this decision, constitutes the kind of wilfullness or recklessness which may result in serious repercussions.[12]

JUDGE WINMILL'S MESSAGE TO THE BAR

Judge Winmill here gives the plaintiff Scentsy a clear warning: either improve your retention and preservation policies now, or I will be even tougher against you if this ever comes up again in a future case in my court. This also constitutes a warning to all litigants who may come into Judge Winmill's court—or to any court that follows his commonsense approach.

Judge Winmill goes on to make a point of emphasizing his displeasure of the plaintiff's slipshod preservation. All judges are like that, as well they should be. Justice needs the facts and evidence. If one side

---

[12] *Id.* at *9.

destroys the evidence—either on purpose or by negligence—and the other side does not, then it gives the negligent side an unfair advantage. Judges must keep the courts balanced and fair. That is why judges are angered by negligent preservation. All lawyers should be intense, even to the point of rudeness, to try to force their clients to take not only basic reasonable efforts, but best efforts, to save the truth. This will earn you the respect of the presiding judge and give you some leeway when some mistakes are inevitably made.

Obviously, best practices were not employed here. Judge Winmill responds as you would expect.

> While it is unlikely that relevant documents were destroyed, we can never be certain. That uncertainty, which can only be attributed to Scentsy's inadequate retention policies and litigation hold, is very troubling to the Court. Moreover, the Court views spoliation as a very serious matter with potentially serious consequences for the parties. Accordingly, the Court has, in essence, sanctioned Scentsy by requiring it to pay the deposition costs as outlined above, and by giving Scentsy a shot across the bow that if there is evidence that spoliation occurred, future consequences will be harsh.[13]

CONCLUSION

Lawyers should engage in preservation activities in every case. Although you can agree with opposing counsel to forgo e-discovery in a case and not search for or produce clients' ESI (and believe it or not, many lawyers still do that), you cannot agree to forgo preservation. No lawyers admit that they do that, although some may informally agree not to look too closely at each other's preservation. If one side screws up, the other side is likely to use that to their advantage to press for sanctions.

Of course, you cannot complain about the other side's failures if your side has also screwed up. You must have your own preservation house in order before you can attack and get anywhere with it. Otherwise, you are likely to have the judge throw up his or her hands and say, "A pox on both your houses!"

---

[13] *Id.*

This is exactly what Judge Lucy Koh did when she entered adverse inference sanctions against both Apple and Samsung for failure to preserve ESI.[14] It is well worth reading to see how both sides screwed up preservation in the hottest case in the country back in 2012. The spoliation issues were not settled until just a few days before the trial began. I am sure that the trial lawyers on both sides could have done without those distractions.

All good lawyers these days are concerned with their clients' preservation of ESI. They do not want their case to be over before it even gets started. The dark clouds of looming spoliation can do that. Thus, strong preservation efforts are necessary in every case.

In EDBP, we have identified three basic preservation attorney tasks: hold notices, interviews, and collections. They are the second, third, and fourth steps in the 10-step attorney workflow. These preservation activities should ideally all flow out of the first step of litigation readiness. *Scentsy* demonstrates the importance of this. They should also be connected with the fifth cooperation step. Disclosure of preservation at a Rule 26(f) conference is contemplated by the rules. This forces any objections and, if none are made, can protect a party from later attack.

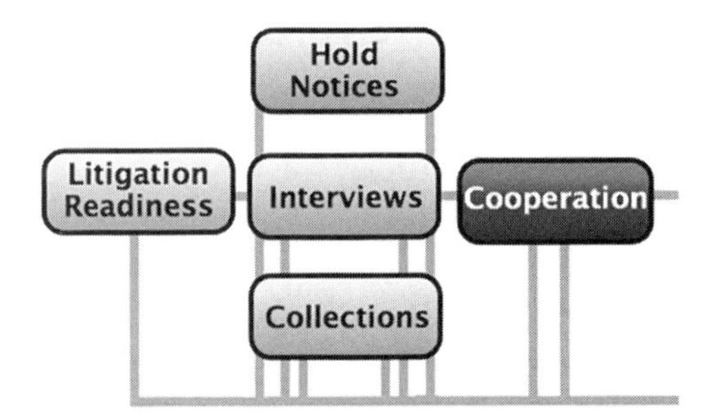

Here is an outline from *www.EDBP.com* of these preservation activities:

- Hold notices
  - Notify custodians
  - Notify information technology (IT)
  - Preserve in place

[14] Apple v. Samsung, U.S.D.C., N.D. Ca., Case No.: 11-CV-01846-LHK, Document 1894 (Aug. 21, 2012).

- Witness interviews
- Collections
  - Self-collection
  - Bulk collection by IT
  - Cross-border issues (when international ESI collection is involved)

As a concluding comment, I would like to emphasize the importance of applying the proportionality doctrine to preservation. Some cases are so small and notice is so premature (as is typical, for instance, in a pre-suit employee equal opportunity charge) that only the bare minimum preservation activities are required. The only thing that might be proportional for some cases is to send out a written hold notice, and nothing more. It may be sufficient to just instruct key custodians to preserve in place and not alter or destroy specified information. Immediate interviews and collection activities might not be required. In other cases, you might want to notify and interview, but defer any collection.

There is no one-size-fits-all reasonable response that is appropriate for every case, or even every type of case. There is only a minimum standard of putting notices in writing. A carefully crafted litigation hold policy should specify proportional efforts, not require all-out efforts for every suit. Beyond the written notice, it all depends on the facts and proportionality analysis. That is where a skilled and experienced attorney is worth a thousand new lit-hold software programs. It is the carpenter, not the hammer, who builds the house of holds. Of course, it is nice to have good software, too. Any carpenter still stuck with a handsaw spreadsheet to track lit-holds will tell you that.

10

Wreck-It Ralph: Things in e-Discovery that I Want to Destroy!

It is rare to see popular media use my name, Ralph. The last I recall is the famous Jackie Gleason character, Ralph Kramden. So when a Disney movie, *Wreck-It Ralph,* came out staring a video game character named Ralph, I decided to embrace the questionable image of Ralph as a wrecker. This chapter will list three things in e-discovery that I think should be wrecked—things that stand as obstructions to future progress.

DISTRUST

There is too much distrust between attorneys when it comes to electronic discovery. Because of this lack of trust, there is lack of cooperation. Instead, there is obstruction and needless bickering. It all flows out of lack of trust.

With a few rare exceptions (e.g., when opposing counsel is a known discovery predator), there is no good reason to automatically assume that the other side is trying to hide the ball. Certainly, opposing counsel's use of advanced technology should not, in itself, be a cause for distrust. I remember when I was the first lawyer to have a computer. Other lawyers did not distrust me because of that. They may have smiled at my crazy hobby or asked me many questions, but they did not distrust me. The same comments apply to keyword search. Why is there continued distrust of today's advanced software and predictive coding? There is no good reason, except perhaps the deterioration of civility in society as a whole. The legal profession must not let the screaming heads in the media pollute our noble profession. You should argue vigorously on legal points, but after the trial, have a beer together and get to know your fellow lawyer.

In the old days of paper-only productions, no one ever thought they had the right to audit the other side's production. You trusted that they did their job—that the attorneys were fair and honest. You did not assume that they were trying to hide the ball as a matter of course. You did not ask for detailed disclosure from the responding party as to how they searched for paper records. You did not ask to be shown documents that were deemed irrelevant. Such requests would have been laughed at.

There was trust then, and there should be trust now—not trust *and* verify. The verify part—the tell-me-what-you-did part—only arose in the past if there was evidence of hiding the ball, either intentionally or by negligence. You did not just distrust lawyers, or the opposing parties they represented, until you had some objective reason to do so. Now, far too many lawyers think they have a right to audit before there is any cause to do so. They think they have a right to see samples of irrelevant documents. Where in the rules does it allow that? (Answer: nowhere!) We need to wreck this kind of paranoia. We need to wreck these overreaching, fear-based demands for disclosure.

The rules of discovery are based on trust and the imposition of sanctions by judges when that trust is betrayed. We need to wreck distrust. We need to go back to the rules. We need to go back to the kind of cooperation between parties that can only develop when there is a foundation of trust.

LAW FIRMS RUNNING SIDE BUSINESSES UNDER THE GUISE OF LITIGATION SUPPORT

Why are law firms running little e-discovery vendor operations under the guise of litigation support departments with their clients as captive customers? The core competence of lawyers and law firms is legal services. That is what they should stick to. Most law firms and corporate law departments should wreck (or at least severely curtail) their litigation support departments. They should outsource almost everything they do to vendors who specialize in that kind of work.[1]

The processing of ESI, collection of ESI, creation and maintenance of ESI databases, software hosting of ESI, and technical support are all nonlegal business functions. They are highly technical and complex tasks. No one can argue that these are legal services, as the recent cases under Section 1920 for award of court costs show.[2] Yet, most large and even medium-sized law firms today think they can and should operate such a business. The law firm management apparently thinks it is just like making paper photocopies. They are wrong and this misapprehension should be wrecked.

Some think it is a good way to make money. This is wrong again, and this notion should be wrecked. Think about the ethics of that. Think about the liability of running such a business with your clients—to whom you are a fiduciary—as your only customers, and captive customers at that.

Some think that they have to use their own people to do these technical services because no one else out there can do it right. That may have been true many years ago, but not anymore; this notion too should be wrecked. There are plenty of vendors out there who are as good, if not better, than your department. They are probably less expensive, too. Are you afraid to lose institutional knowledge? The vendors you outsource to would probably be glad to hire your experienced people. Indeed, if outsourcing is done right, no one should lose a job and it all can stay in country. This outsourcing is only about outsourcing nonlegal services from a law firm to a business that specializes in such services.

The fundamental notion that all law firms are competent to run an e-discovery business should also be wrecked. Most are not competent

---

[1] *See* Ralph Losey, *Five Reasons to Outsource Litigation Support* (LTN Nov. 2, 2012).

[2] 28 USC §1920; Race Tires Am., Inc. v. Hoosier Racing Tire Corp., 674 F.3d 158, 167 (3d Cir. 2012).

to run any business, much less a complex, highly technical, capital-intensive business such as nonlegal e-discovery services. Most are providing their clients with second-class services, often at a higher price than most e-discovery vendors. Wreck it. Leave the nonlegal services to vendors.

If you are the very rare firm that has a great little e-discovery operation set up in your law firm, then don't wreck it. However, do consider spinning it off to a separate for-profit business where it belongs. Then, you will find out how good it really is.

VENDORS WHO PRACTICE LAW

Lest you think I am too vendor friendly, there are many things about vendors I would like to wreck, too. In addition to their Byzantine pricing structures, I would like to wreck their experts who go around practicing law without a license. Vendors who encroach on law firm turf and provide legal services should be wrecked—and wrecked hard.

Only practicing lawyers are permitted by law to provide legal advice. Vendors never can. They may have lawyers working for them as employees. They may even have the requisite legal expertise. However, they are not law firms and they cannot give legal advice—end of story. Some do anyway under the guise of providing *technology* advice or *educational information.* The line has become way too blurry. I want to wreck the blurry line. I want to make it a clear and bright line again.

When computer technology and software was young, IBM salespeople never gave legal advice. Neither did Westlaw or Lexis. The state bars who regulate the unauthorized practice of law (UPL) have become lax in recent years, especially when it comes to e-discovery vendors. After all, the vendors keep poaching law firms' best and brightest in e-discovery. Many, if not most, law firms today are adrift and in desperate need of good legal advice in this area. Naturally, they turn to the vendors, as that is where many of the tech-savvy lawyers are. However, this has to stop. It is unhealthy and wrong on so many levels. All of the good vendors know it and are trying to stop. I applaud the activity of the DC Bar to take first steps to try to curb e-discovery vendor UPL.[3] The unauthorized practice of law is a crime in most states. It is about time for vendors who cross that line to be prosecuted.

Do you still think that I'm biased in favor of vendors? I am an equal opportunity wrecker. Law firms should outsource their business services to vendors. Vendors, in turn, should outsource their legal practice back to where it once belonged. Yes, we need to work together as a team, but each member needs to know his or her role.

In the *Wreck-It Ralph* movie, Ralph caused havoc by changing games and trying to be what he was not. We need to learn from that and stick to our own games—what we know and do best.

CONCLUSION

If you study any field of human endeavor, you will see many things done wrong—things that you would like to change. Electronic discovery is no exception. This chapter lists just three of those things. In truth, they are not even my top three (although they are close). There are many more things in e-discovery that should be wrecked. Among them is the stubborn refusal of most attorneys to embrace e-discovery and take the

---

[3] Doherty, *D.C. Bar Calls Out E-Discovery Vendors in the District* (LTN July 12, 2012).

time to really learn how to do it. I continue to be amazed at how many lawyers still see e-discovery as optional, believing that paper discovery is enough.

I would also like to see the traditional Go Fish keyword search negotiations wrecked. You should always test keywords before you use them, not just blindly guess. Yet, this practice still goes on across America in case after case. The linear review of documents is another thing I'd like to wreck. The same goes for all of the myths out there about predictive coding, such as the following:

- It should only be used in the biggest cases or in certain kinds of cases.
- It is a brand new technology and there is no proof that it works.
- It is just based on a very big "bag of words" model that excludes semantic and grammatical analysis.
- Courts will not approve using it (this one is really archaic in view of all of the courts that have approved it).
- It is not defensible (or at least, it is hard to defend) and will require an expensive *Daubert* hearing.
- It misses hot documents.
- It takes a long time to do.
- It is expensive.
- You have to give up your confidentiality rights to use it.
- Lawyer judgment is replaced by machine learning.
- The computer is always right.
- It is the only kind of search you need to do (mono-modal).
- Vendors do the search for you.
- The TREC Legal Track has established standards and best practices for predictive coding use.
- You have to reach a certain recall level before you can say that predictive coding has worked.
- It is a defense trap or a plaintiff's trap.

The list of predictive coding myths and misinformation goes on and on.

I would also like to wreck the notion that the electronic discovery reference model (EDRM) is the one and only viable model to understand e-discovery. I do not want to wreck EDRM itself; it is a great model and has its place—an important place. It is an especially good place to start. I just want to wreck the strange idea (not endorsed by EDRM itself) that it is the one and only model. In fact, I am actively working on wrecking this idea by creating another model that tracks legal services only and does not include what vendors do.[4]

Yes, we are back to that blurry line again, which I would like to see made clear and bright. There should be no more switching from game to game, which, in these now blurry days of e-discovery, is a real game-changer.

[4] *See http://www.EDBP.com.*

11 Confessions of a Trekkie

I am a Star Trek addict—a true nerd. I have loved Star Trek since I was a kid in the 1960s watching the television show with my parents. We all loved the show, even if it was sometimes challengingly liberal for my conservative parents. I have seen every Star Trek show ever made, multiple times. I have even bought several Star Trek video games, just so I could have the personal thrill of firing phasers (on stun, of course) and a full volley of photon torpedoes (not on stun). *Make it so.* Fight the Borg. Save the universe.

I share all of this with you so that you will understand why my new favorite judge is Otis D. Wright, II. Judge Wright is a U.S. District Judge in California who appears to be a Star Trek addict, too. He wrote an interesting opinion with many Trekkie references when ruling on a discovery violation.[1] *Ingenuity* is a bizarre copyright case involving copyright trolls (*Ferengi* might be the better word for them).

Judge Wright's opinion begins with this famous quote from Spock in *Star Trek II: The Wrath of Khan* (1982): "The needs of the many outweigh the needs of the few."

---

[1]Ingenuity 13 LLC v. Doe, No. 2:12-CV-. 8333 (ODW), 2013 WL 1898633 (C.D. Cal. May 6, 2012).

Thinking of the scene in *Wrath of Khan* where Spock utters these fateful words nearly brings a tear to my eye; no doubt, it did for the plaintiffs here, too. It was a warning shot that they were about to be phaser-blasted—or as lawyers say these days, "bench slapped." The first paragraph of the opinion gives a great summary of the plaintiffs, *Ferengi* all, and includes a reference to my favorite Star Trek villain, the Borg:

> Plaintiffs have outmaneuvered the legal system. They've discovered the nexus of antiquated copyright laws, paralyzing social stigma, and unaffordable defense costs. And they exploit this anomaly by accusing individuals of illegally downloading a single pornographic video. Then they offer to settle—for a sum calculated to be just below the cost of a bare-bones defense. For these individuals, resistance is futile; most reluctantly pay rather than have their names associated with illegally downloading porn. So now, copyright laws originally designed to compensate starving artists allow, starving attorneys in this electronic-media era to plunder the citizenry.[2]

Isn't that a terrific beginning to an opinion? But wait, there's more. Judge Wright goes on to say:

> Plaintiffs do have a right to assert their intellectual-property rights, so long as they do it right. But Plaintiffs' filing of cases using the same boilerplate complaint against dozens of defendants raised the Court's alert. It was when the Court realized Plaintiffs engaged their cloak of shell companies and fraud that the Court went to battlestations.

Battlestations, battlestations! Can you not hear the classic Star Trek alarms in your head? The judge then goes on with another first by using a Google Earth photo to expose a plaintiff's lawyer's lie.

Plaintiffs had stated that a defendant lived in a large mansion with a big gate out front, whereas the Google Earth photo showed it to be a typical small suburban tract home—no gate, no mansion. This was just

---

[2] *Id.*

one example of Judge Wright's exposure of a pattern of lies by the plaintiffs' counsel. It led to his dismissal of the case, award of fees to the defendants, and—declaring that these particular plaintiff's counsel *suffer from a form of moral turpitude unbecoming of an officer of the court*—referring them all to state and federal bar associations for ethics investigations.

But wait, there are still more torpedoes left in the Captain's—I mean, the Judge's—arsenal. Judge Wright concluded his sanctions with an awesome flurry of weapons fire, reminiscent of Kirk himself:

> Third, though Plaintiffs boldly probe the outskirts of law, the only enterprise they resemble is RICO. The federal agency eleven decks up is familiar with their prime directive and will gladly refit them for their next voyage. The Court will refer this matter to the United States Attorney for the Central District of California. The [Court] will also refer this matter to the Criminal Investigation Division of the Internal Revenue Service and will notify all judges before whom these attorneys have pending cases. For the sake of completeness, the Court requests Pietz to assist by filing a report, within 14 days, containing contact information for: (1) every bar (state and federal) where these attorneys are admitted to practice; and (2) every judge before whom these attorneys have pending cases.

Judge Otis Wright, you are a true Trekkie and my new hero. Thanks for a great order. I cannot wait to cite it against certain Klingon-like opposing counsel I know.

POSTSCRIPT

According to the Wikipedia entry on this infamous Prenda law firm, the attorneys dissolved the firm shortly after the adverse ruling.[3] Thereafter, these attorneys were hit with a series of fines and indictments.[4] Prenda and attorney Paul Hansmeier filed an "emergency motion" in the Ninth Circuit seeking a stay of Judge Wright's sanctions order.

---

[3] *See https://en.wikipedia.org/wiki/Prenda_Law.*

[4] *Id. Also see, How Two California Solos Helped Take Down "Porn Troll" Prenda Law,* ABA J. LAW NEWS (Jan. 14, 2014).

It was denied without prejudice to the sanctioned parties' right to request a stay in Judge Wright's court. They then filed an ex parte motion seeking a stay from Wright. On May 21, 2013, Wright responded by ordering each sanctioned party (Steele, Duffy, Hansmeier, Gibbs, AF Holdings, Ingenuity 13, and Prenda) to pay an additional $1,000 per day (to the clerk of the court), on top of the previously ordered $81,319.72 payable to John Doe's attorneys, until all sanctions were fully paid.

Meanwhile, on May 20, 2013, attorneys Steele, Hansmeier, and Duffy had secured and posted a bond of $101,650 on behalf of themselves, Prenda Law Inc., Ingenuity 13 LLC, and AF Holdings LLC (but not Gibbs), to guarantee payment of Judge Wright's sanctions order if upheld on appeal. The amount of the bond was later raised to a total of $237,584 to cover a possible attorney fee award on appeal. The appeal of the bond order was denied by the Ninth Circuit.

Oral argument in the Ninth Circuit on the merits took place on May 4, 2015. The video recording of the argument can be found on the Ninth Circuit website.[5] The Ninth Circuit[6] ruled on June 10, 2016 and affirmed the lower court's phaser blasts. They found that under the circumstances of this case the sanctions were well within the court's inherent authority.

[5] *See http://www.ca9.uscourts.gov/media/view_video.php?pk_vid=0000007584. See also https://www.youtube.com/watch?v=m37QqmBU7Dc* (where it has over 4,000 views).

[6] *See https://scholar.google.com/scholar_case?case=11989151700240198059 &hl.*

Courts Struggle with Determining Reasonability of e-Discovery Vendor Bills

12

A case in one of my favorite fields of substantive law, *qui tam*, provides a good illustration of a court struggling with e-discovery vendor prices.[1] District Court Judge Sam A. Lindsay in Dallas had to determine the reasonability of the prevailing plaintiff's attorney fees and the reasonability of the charges of their vendor, UHY Advisors. UHY is a large accounting firm who has what they call an "e-discovery and digital forensic team." The issue was not scope and entitlement, as you would see under a 28 USC §1920 court costs award. The plaintiff was entitled to reimbursement of costs under the substantive statute.[2] For this reason, the primary issue here was reasonability of the costs award.

Judge Lindsay had no problem with analysis of reasonable attorneys' fees, an issue with which he has long experience, but the issue of e-discovery costs reasonability was new and vexatious, much like the lawsuit itself. That

---

[1]United States ex rel. Becker v. Tools & Metals, Inc., No. 3:05-CV-0627-L, 2013 U.S. Dist. LEXIS 46529 (N.D. Tex. Mar. 31, 2013).

[2]31 U.S.C. §3730(d)(1)-(2) (a qui tam plaintiff "shall ... receive an amount for reasonable expenses which the court finds to have been necessarily incurred, plus reasonable attorneys' fees and costs.")

may be one reason Judge Lindsay was clearly upset by all of these motions and ended his opinion with these pointed comments:

> This litigation has become protracted; however, at some point all litigation must come to an end. Considerable but scarce judicial resources have been expended.... Accordingly, except for a clerical error, a matter relating to any supplemental fee request, or an intervening change in the law, the court is not inclined to discuss or write further on the issue of attorney's fees and costs in this action. The parties are aware of their appellate options, which they should exercise if they believe that the court has ruled contrary to law, but litigation will end at this level. In this vein, if any motion is filed for reconsideration or to amend or alter the judgment, and the court finds such motion is without merit or good cause to be lacking, the court will impose monetary sanctions against the offending attorney or party. The parties are strongly warned not to test the court patience in this regard.

QUI TAM, ABRAHAM LINCOLN, AND ME

Before I go into the problem of determining vendor price reasonability and how Judge Lindsay and his magistrate Judge Renee Harris Toliver handled it, a little background on the esoteric field of *qui tam* law is in order. The law is ancient in origin, going back a thousand years to the early days of common law in England. The first *qui tam* law allowed a person to turn in another for poaching game on the king's land and get paid a bounty for the action. Over the centuries, this morphed into a lawsuit in which a private citizen could sue in the name of the government for any fraud against the government. If they prevailed, the citizen would receive part of any recovery and the government would get the rest.

This part of our common law was reinvigorated in the United States by one of my favorite lawyers, Abraham Lincoln. He had legislation passed based on the old common law that encouraged whistleblowers to come forward with knowledge of fraudulent billing of the federal government during the Civil War. There was a lot of fraudulent billing at that time (and there still is) and President Lincoln was desperate to try to stop it.

Today, the federal and state laws implementing *qui tam* are called False Claims Acts. It is one of the most complex and bizarre areas of law in the United States, which, I suppose, is one reason I specialized in it for a time before moving full-time to e-discovery in 2006. It is almost as complex as my other area of specialty, the dreaded field of Employee Retirement Income Security Act of 1974 (ERISA) litigation.

Without spending too much more of your valuable time on *qui tam*, suffice it to say that these are very complex cases with many factual issues involving fraud, sometimes including intentional criminal activities. These are lawsuits where an individual sues in the name of the government (*ex rel.*). The cases are filed under seal and the defendants are not even told of the lawsuit until after the government has had a chance to investigate the allegations. The cases often remain shrouded in grand jury secrecy with related criminal investigations by U.S. Attorneys and the Federal Bureau of Investigation, among others. (That is one reason why I cannot speak about most of my experiences for *both sides* in this sometimes exciting area of the law.)

If the government thinks a private whistleblower's case has merit, they may take all or part of it over and prosecute the case for the relator (the private plaintiff). If the government wins, the relator gets a share of the recovery, typically from between 10 percent to 15 percent, plus an award of the relator's reasonable attorney fees and costs. This brings us back to the question of reasonable e-discovery costs in *United States ex rel. Becker v. Tools & Metals, Inc.*

WHAT IS A REASONABLE CHARGE FOR NONLEGAL E-DISCOVERY SERVICES?

Most courts have great difficulty determining whether e-discovery vendor charges are reasonable. After all, most law firms and litigants have the same problem. Therefore, it should come as no surprise that judges do too—most of whom have never had *any* experience retaining vendors before they went on the bench.

Before I tell you what the actual charges were here and what the judges decided, try coming up with a ballpark figure of what a reasonable charge would be. The information provided in the opinion is pretty sparse, but it should give you enough information for some ballpark estimates. Please remember, these are all just vendor charges and do not include any attorney fees or accounting fees, just nonlegal e-discovery services.

Before you guess a number, consider this additional background. The lawsuit started on March 25, 2005, as two cases that were later consolidated into one. The cases were against multiple defendants involving complex issues related to false billings for tools used on military aircraft, including the F-22 and the F-35 fighter jets. The primary culprit, TMI, filed for bankruptcy. The chief executive officer (CEO) of TMI, Todd Loftis, was charged criminally for the scheme, found guilty, and sentenced to seven years in prison. The case continued against deeper pockets who were alleged to have recklessly supervised the inflated charges of their subcontractor, TMI.

The government intervened in several of the counts, but not all. After the primary defendants survived a motion for summary judgment, the case settled in April 2012 for $15.8 million. The two relators, John Becker and Robert Spencer, received a $2 million share of that settlement. Judge Lindsay also awarded another $1,675,323.28 to them for reasonable attorney fees. He also awarded the relators' costs, almost all of which were e-discovery related. (The intervening government did not receive a fee or cost award.)

To summarize, we know this was a very complex case involving many entities and witnesses that went on for more than seven years and ended up settling for over $18 million. Have a guess yet as to the total e-discovery expenses? Would you assume more than $10 million? $5 million? $2 million? Less than $1 million? Make a guess, and then read on for descriptions from the opinion on the e-discovery billings. See how it changes your estimate.

E-DISCOVERY CHARGES IN *BECKER*

Here is the first fact that should impact your analysis. Although the case went on for seven years, a majority of the costs at issue were for services performed by UHY from February 1, 2010, through May 31, 2011—just a year and a quarter. No doubt you are now adjusting your costs estimate downward a bit. Now consider these additional facts from the opinion:

- The e-discovery charges included "processing and uploading" data and the "creation of a relativity index." Yes, that means Relativity review software was used.
- The plaintiffs' purchased six user accounts.
- The data was hosted by UHY from February 2010 through September 2011.
- The hosting fees were billed at a rate of $39 per gigabyte (GB) per month.
- There was an additional charge to repair broken and corrupt files received from defendants and to reprocess, upload, and create a search index for the corrupt data.
- UHY used two examiners to image dozens of hard drives of TMI at TMI's offices.
- UHY provided a project manager dedicated solely to the case.

Now what do you think UHY charged the plaintiff relators for all of these services? Ok, I know what you are thinking: "How many gigabytes were involved? How many files? How many custodians? Give us at least some idea of the volume of the data so we can make a more educated estimate. After all, you did tell us the gigabyte hosting charge of $39 per month." Sorry, apparently Judge Lindsay did not consider that information important enough to include anywhere in his 52-page opinion, which included 17 footnotes. However, we are told that *dozens* of hard drives were imaged. Furthermore, a close study of the opinion (and a little reverse engineering) does show that the size of the data hosted was just over 500 GB (19,739.30/39), or 506 GBs to be exact. So, again I ask you to formulate an educated guess as to what UHY charged its customer for all of these services and what amount the judge approved as reasonable.

CONFLICTING EVIDENCE OF REASONABILITY OF DATA PROCESSING CHARGES

In total, UHY charged its client about $900,000 in this case. So, if you guessed around $1 million, you were about right. I suspect that many of you guessed a much higher amount. The entire amount the vendor charged in this case was not awarded for a variety of reasons that we will get into. First, let us break down these charges into their component parts as Judge Lindsay did in his opinion, starting with the data processing and Relativity review platform creation fees.

UHY charged $299,710.34 for processing, uploading, and creating the Relativity database for 506 GB of documents. UHY charged an additional $38,116.38 to repair broken or corrupt files produced by defendants and reprocess them, for a total charge for the processing and uploading of $299,710.34. That works out to about $592 per GB. Does that seem reasonable to you? Remember this was incurred in 2010 and 2011. The vendor supported the reasonability of these charges with an affidavit by Douglas Herman, Managing Director of e-Discovery and Digital Forensics Practice at UHY Advisors. In the court's words:

> Herman states in his declaration that the fees charged by UHY are consistent with market rates and fees charged to UHY's other customers based on the level of service it provided to Spencer over more than 28 months.

The defendants attacked the affidavit, basically saying it was self-serving and that the vendor had a vested interest in the outcome of the decision. They also submitted an opposing affidavit by an expert in the field, George Socha. What do you think George opined was a reasonable fee to process, upload, and create a Relativity review platform of 506 gigabytes? Here is what the court said about the Socha affidavit:

> Lockheed presented affidavit testimony of George Socha, the president of a company that provides e-discovery consulting and expert services, who opined that a reasonable fee for the services provided by UHY would be $20,000.

This works out to be $39.53 per gigabyte. Did anyone guess that low? Did you think the vendor here overcharged the customer 15 times too much ($300,000 instead of $20,000)? Do you think that $280,000 of their $300,000 charge was unreasonable?

Apparently, the affidavit and defendant's other arguments did not convince Magistrate Judge Renee Toliver, who awarded the plaintiffs $174,395.97 for these services, which works out to $344.66 per GB.

In other words, Judge Toliver reduced the vendor's bill from $299,710 to $174,396, a reduction of $125,314.

Judge Lindsay agreed with his magistrate and rejected the defendant's opposition as "purely speculative" and "not supported by the evidence." This seems a bit harsh to me, considering there were affidavits from two respected experts, but here is Judge Lindsay's holding:

> Moreover, Lockheed's contention that the actual cost of uploading and creating a search index "*may have been substantially less*" than the magistrate judge's $174,395.97 estimate is purely speculative and not supported by evidence. Further, a court necessarily must rely on its measured discretion when presented with conflicting evidence. Frankly, this type of determination does not lend itself to mathematical precision; and the court finds the magistrate judge's decision is within the bounds of reasonableness.

The judges' reasoning for the $125,314 haircut they gave the vendor here is quite curious. They did not challenge at all the reasonability of the vendor's charges. Instead, they reduced the cost award because they held that the plaintiffs should never have paid anything to the vendor to repair the broken or corrupt files produced by the defendants. Instead, they should have asked the defendants to produce the files again, but this time have the files produced right. In other words, they attacked the necessity of fixing corrupt files and reprocessing them, not the reasonability of the expenses. Again, this shows a fair degree of naiveté in my opinion, as there are always corrupt files in any production. It also is highly unlikely that a request to the defendants, including a bankrupt entity whose CEO was in jail, would have succeeded. Still, that was their reasoning.

Based on this holding, it seems to me that this case now provides legal authority to argue that a producing party has a duty to fix all troublesome files they produce to you. What a host of arguments those demands will make as each side blames the other on technical issues. The judges then went on to figure that this unnecessary repair cost justified what they called an approximate "one-third" reduction in the vendor's total processing and uploading costs. (It was actually a

42 percent reduction, not 33 percent, but perhaps I quibble.) Here is Judge Lindsay's holding:

> Based on the foregoing determination, the magistrate judge deducted the $38,116.38 allegedly incurred to repair broken or corrupt files produced by Lockheed. She also reduced the amount sought by deducting for reprocessing costs. Because Spencer's billing records did not segregate the costs for reprocessing and uploading the data and creating a searchable index, the magistrate judge estimated that one-third of time billed by UHY was for reprocessing, one-third for was for uploading, and one-third was for creating an index and concluded that Spencer should only recover two-thirds of the time billed by UHY totaling $174,395.97 for uploading and creating an index. The magistrate therefore reduced the total amount sought ($299,710.34) by $125,314.17, which is slightly more than 30 percent of the total amount sought. Based on the court's review of and familiarity with the record, evidence, and applicable law, and the magistrate judge's determination that Herman's testimony should be discounted rather than excluded, the court finds no error in the magistrate's determination.

REASONABILITY OF DATA HOSTING CHARGES

That takes care of the processing and uploading fees, but what about the hosting and other vendor fees? The vendor here charged $424,289 for hosting for 20 months and an additional $15,750 for six user fees. The defendants argued none of these hosting and user fees should be awarded—not because the $39.53 per gigabyte per month hosting fee was too high a charge or the $2,625 user fee was too high, but because the plaintiffs only used 5 of the 506 GB worth of documents so hosted and accessed. This was a novel argument, but the court did not find it persuasive:

> Lockheed contends that UHY billing Spencer $440,039 for hosting of and user access to the documents produced in the litigation is unreasonable under the circumstances because Spencer used only five of these documents during the litigation and did not notice a single deposition.

> The court disagrees with Lockheed's contention that reasonableness is determined based on the number of documents used in the litigation. Due to increasing amounts of electronic documents being created by individuals and companies and the relative ease of retrieving such documents, discovery in complex commercial cases such as this has evolved into an extensive undertaking with parties producing and culling through large quantities of electronic documents to identify key documents that will ultimately be used to establish a claim or defense. Many of the documents produced and reviewed in such cases are never used in the litigation. This, however, does not necessarily mean that the documents do not have to be reviewed by the parties for relevance by physically examining them or through the use of litigation software with searching capability to assist parties in identifying key documents. Lockheed's objection in this regard is therefore without merit.

These are wise observations by Judge Lindsay. Once again, the arguments made by defendants here were really attacking the necessity of doing e-discovery at all, not the reasonability of charges. Of course, you have to look at documents to determine the truth of what happened in a dispute. This is particularly true of *qui tam* cases where you are dealing with fraudulent billing.

The district and magistrate judges did, however, reduce the hosting and user access fees totaling $440,039 to $271,110.23. Once again, they did not do so by examining the charges that other vendors make for hosting Relativity databases. They did not find the $39.53 per gigabyte per month hosting fee to be too high, nor the $2,625 for 20 months of user access fees to be too high. Instead, they reduced the award by reducing the time period that the data should have been hosted and cutting out one of the five user fees.

The judges reduced the time because they held that the plaintiffs should have closed the database as soon as a settlement was announced in principle, not waited seven months until the deal actually closed. They cut one of the six user fees because they said the time records submitted showed that only five people ever used Relativity, so the purchase of six user licenses was unnecessary.

The plaintiff's protests that this was all hindsight and second-guessing, were rejected. In fact, Judge Lindsay found the plaintiff's argument regarding the danger of closing the Relativity platform before the settlement was finalized to be rather *snarky* and chastised the plaintiff's counsel:

> The court preliminarily notes that it does not appreciate the unprofessional and condescending tone of counsel's declaration. Further, while Spencer states in his motion that it would have been "time consuming and costly" to remove and reload the data if settlement was not reached and his counsel states, "[t]he estimated costs of nearly $100,000 for an unloading, storing and reloading process was a large obligation to incur," both statements are conclusory and unsupported by credible evidence.

In fact, I do not think any prudent lawyer would have closed the platform right away and risked that expense. However, the cost amount does seem inflated to me.

REASONABILITY OF DATA COLLECTION CHARGES

The next cost at issue was for the vendor's ESI extraction or forensic imaging of TMI's hard drives and related travel costs ($104,716.10). The defendants argued that it was unreasonable in comparison to the amount of money they spent for similar services. Here is how Judge Lindsay summarizes the parties interesting argument on this cost:

> Spencer countered that the expenses were reasonable because the services performed by UHY were different than those performed by Lockheed's vendor. Spencer contended that UHY provided two examiners to image dozens of hard drives at a fixed cost per hard drive for a total of $61,890; the cost of the associated media was $12,750; and related travel costs were $10,206.10. In its reply brief, Lockheed contended that Spencer's approach was to copy everything regardless of whether it was relevant, whereas Lockheed's vendor, based on information obtained from the Government's investigation, conducted a targeted extraction of information from the TMI hard drives,

> which resulted in their imaging less than a dozen documents and avoiding extraction of large quantities of irrelevant documents belonging to employees who were not involved in the fraud.

The court agreed with the defendants on that argument and only awarded $20,000 for copying of TMI's hard drives:

> The Court finds particularly persuasive the Lockheed Defendants' argument that Spencer could have conducted a more targeted search for relevant documents, thereby saving considerable time and associated expense. Spencer's course of action was not prudent under the circumstances, considering that he could have conducted depositions to determine how best to conduct more limited discovery, rather than copy all materials even those that were highly unlikely to contain relevant information.

In response to the plaintiffs' argument that "there was no one to depose because TMI was bankrupt and had been dissolved for many years and Loftis, TMI's former president, was in federal prison," Judge Lindsay pointed out that there are technological alternatives that make it possible to make a more targeted collection. Although I am not sure this really would have saved money here and most experts would make forensic images when a fraudster going to prison is involved, the $61,890 charge was still very high. Judge Lindsay's observations are interesting and should be noted and followed in most cases:

> [Plaintiff's argument] fails to address why he was unable to conduct a targeted search of the hard drives through the use of key word searches or having UHY provide a map of the hard drives to assist in the preliminary identification of key words or areas that might contain relevant information. With the availability of technology and the capability of e-discovery vendors today in this area, the court concludes that it was unreasonable for Spencer to simply image all of the hard drives without at least first considering or attempting a more targeted and focused extraction. Also, lack of familiarity with technology in this regard is not an excuse and does not relieve parties or their

> attorneys of their duty to ensure that the services performed and fees charged by third party vendors are reasonable, particularly when recovery of such expenses is sought in litigation. The court therefore overrules this objection.

Although I do not think keyword search is the answer, especially at the collection phase, targeted collections are always in order. Attorneys certainly do have a duty to ensure that the services performed and fees charged by third-party vendors are reasonable.

REASONABILITY OF PROJECT MANAGEMENT CHARGES

The vendor here added one more charge to their bill: $38,514.48 for project management costs. These costs were completely disallowed by the court, primarily because there was no description on the bills of the services provided, nor was there any reason provided for why the project required a full-time project manager. With a little more thought on the vendor's part here, they probably would have received at least some award for project management services. We all know how important these services usually are.

CONCLUSION

The plaintiff's vendor in this case charged a total of $880,705 for e-discovery services: $299,710.34 for data processing, $440,039 for hosting, $38,514 for project management, $61,890 for collection, and $40,552.21 for sales tax. The court found those charges to be unreasonably high and instead awarded the plaintiffs $549,281. The arguments on reasonability seemed to have little to do with what you would expect; instead, they were more like arguments concerning the necessity of the services. Where expert testimony was heard on some of the charges, it seemed to have little effect on the court, possibly because of the wide divergence of expert opinion: $299,710.34 versus $20,000.

The reasonability of vendor fees is a new wild-west issue. There are currently few guidelines for practitioners. If you are in the enviable position of the plaintiffs here, you would do well to retain an outside expert to assist you, not just rely on your vendor. The court might, as in this case, tend to disbelieve their opinions as biased and self-serving.

Lawyers might also want to retain an expert to help at the outset of the case when negotiating prices with a vendor for a big project. Judge Lindsay is right: lawyers have a duty to ensure that the services performed and fees charged by third-party vendors are reasonable. If you are a trial lawyer and are confused by the maze of vendor services and charges, get an expert to help you. Even the experts are sometimes mightily confused by vendor games, but e-discovery specialists have the background and experience to figure it out.

Electronic discovery experts can help trial lawyers to select and negotiate a better contract with vendors and help to supervise their performance. The overuse of full forensic examinations in this case is an example of where that supervision would have helped. An outside expert could have devised a more targeted collection scheme or clearly established the necessity. In my experience, vendors often overutilize forensic examinations. After all, they have an economic incentive to do so, and their risk mitigation arguments can be compelling. An outside expert could also have helped in the corrupt files issue in this case. He or she could have determined whether the vendor's additional work was really necessary, or whether a few calls to the producing party could have made that unnecessary as Judge Lindsay seemed to think.

Discussions of reasonability in retaining a vendor, as well as for supporting an award of costs if you win, should reference what other vendors in the area customarily charge for similar services and should have per gigabyte and per file references. These should also be fair "apples-to-apples" comparisons. That is not easy to do, but it is possible. Finally, quality counts. Vendors are like lawyers in that regard. Do you really want to bid out a "bet the company" case to the cheapest professional willing to take it on? There is a lesson in this opinion for vendors, too: provide more details for any project management billings. Ask any lawyer how it is done.

Finally, I issue a plea to vendors: make your billings simpler and easier to understand. Lawyers should not have to hire an impartial outside expert to figure them out. However, in the meantime, until the industry heeds this call, smart lawyers in big cases will do exactly that.

13 A $3.1 Million e-Discovery Vendor Fee Was Reasonable in a $30 Million Case

$3.1 million was found to be a reasonable sum to pay an e-discovery vendor for processing and hosting 2.7 million documents for review in a professional malpractice case.[1] In this case, the plaintiff, a water utility company, sued the engineering firm that designed a 15.5-billion-gallon water reservoir—the largest in Florida. Apparently, the reservoir cracked and leaked and the water company sued everyone involved. Everyone settled, except for the engineers (although, in a bizarre twist, even they *tried* to settle). Although the trial against the remaining defendant, HDR Engineering, took over a month, the jury took less than four hours to rule for the engineers. The prevailing defendant then moved for an award of its reasonable attorney fees and costs. District Court Judge James D. Whittemore, the learned judge who presided over the trial, did not hesitate to award the entire $3.1 million requested for e-discovery expenses.

---

[1]Tampa Bay Water v. HDR Engineering, Inc., Case No. 8:08-CV-2446-T-27TBM. (M.D. Fl. 2012) (also found at 2012 U.S. Dist. LEXIS 157631 and 2012 WL 5387830).

THE 10 PERCENT VENDOR COST WAS PROPORTIONAL AND REASONABLE IN THIS CASE

This $3.1 million award represents a little more than 10 percent of the total value of this case, $30 million. I derive this case value based on the fact that the case actually did settle with HDR for that amount before trial. Then, in a very unusual move (even for Florida), the settlement was later repudiated by the politicians running the plaintiff's water utility, a quasi-governmental authority. I have never seen that happen before. Signed mediation settlement agreements are usually sacrosanct. The case was even dismissed. However, the board was later able to change their mind, reject the deal made at the conclusion of a third mediation, and reopen the case. A majority of the board wanted a trial before a jury, and that is exactly what they got. What a terrible decision.

Judge Whittemore said in his cost order that this case may be the largest engineering professional liability case, in terms of damages sought, ever tried to a jury. At the end of the trial, the plaintiff's lawyers had the gall to ask the jury for a $100 million award. The jury gave them nothing. In denying the motion for new trial, Judge Whittemore found the result unsurprising considering the weakness of the plaintiff's evidence. Tampa Bay Water's case was all wet.

Under these circumstances of a large trial preceded by three years of litigation, the attorney fees and other costs incurred by the defendant HDR were also large. The case docket had 678 entries, including 11 motions to strike, 2 motions to dismiss, 6 motions for protective order, 11 motions to compel, 3 motions to quash, a motion for sanctions, a motion for summary judgment (with two supplements), 4 *Daubert* motions, 29 motions *in limine*, and dozens of nonsubstantive motions.

The defendant was awarded $9,249,219.85 for reasonable attorney fees (almost everything they asked for) and another $7,798,186.22 for other costs incurred, for a total cost and fee award of $20,147,406.07. Therefore, the $3.1 million e-discovery vendor cost was about 15 percent of the total fees and costs incurred by HRD Engineering to defend the case. The judge had no problem finding that to be a reasonable and proportional award.

The plaintiff made a really bad decision to reject the mediated settlement where they would have received a $30 million payment from

HRD Engineering. They not only got a zero verdict but had to pay HRD's fees and costs. Therefore, the citizens of Tampa served by this utility have to pay the bills for the utilities' intransigency. The plaintiff's utility board appealed the decisions on the merits to the Eleventh Circuit, where they lost once again.[2] Shortly after the Eleventh Circuit opinion, Tampa Bay Water finally capitulated and paid the cost award.

ENTITLEMENT TO E-DISCOVERY COST AWARD UNDER CONTRACT, NOT STATUTE

It is important to understand that Judge Whittemore's decision pertained solely to the reasonability of the e-discovery costs incurred. The award was based on a contract that entitled the prevailing party in any litigation arising out of the agreement to receive an award of their reasonable attorney fees and costs. The decision had nothing to do with an award of court costs under 28 USC §1920. The plaintiff tried to attack the award by confusing the two grounds. Judge Whittemore made short work of such a sophistical argument:

> HDR also requests an award of approximately $3.1 million in electronic discovery costs. Tampa Bay Water argues that most of these costs relate to the collection, storage, formatting, coding and organization of electronically stored information ("ESI"), which cannot be taxed as costs. In addressing the taxation of electronic discovery charges under §1920(4), the Third Circuit persuasively reasoned that "only the conversion of native files to TIFF (the agreed-upon default format for production of ESI), and the scanning of documents to create digital duplicates are generally recognized as the taxable 'making copies of material.'" *Race Tires Am., Inc. v. Hoosier Racing Tire Corp.*, 674 F.3d 158, 167 (3d Cir. 2012).
>
> But in this case, the precise scope of § 1920(4) is immaterial because HDR is entitled to recover its reasonable ESI costs under the parties' contract.

---

[2]Tampa Bay Water v. HDR Engineering, Inc., 731 F.3d 1171 (11th Cir. 2013).

This is exactly right. The whole scope of award issue does not arise if the cost award is based on a contract or a statute, as for instance was the case in *United States ex rel. Becker v. Tools & Metals, Inc.*[3] In *Becker,* the award was based on the False Claims Act statute, not the court costs statute.

WHY $3,100,000 FOR E-DISCOVERY VENDOR EXPENSES WAS REASONABLE

Judge Whittemore concisely explains why the sum of $3.1 million was a reasonable amount to pay for e-discovery costs in this case:

> This was a lengthy, highly technical case which involved 17 million pages of documents. Under the circumstances, the electronic discovery costs incurred by HDR were certainly reasonable[15] and necessary in managing this complex, document-intensive case. While a large part of the $3.1 million in ESI costs is attributable to the storage and hosting of ESI, that amount was reasonable and necessary to the effective utilization of ESI in this case. Accordingly, no reductions will be made for the ESI costs incurred by HDR.
>
> [15]To put it in perspective, the total electronic discovery costs would equate to a charge of approximately $0.18 per page for a single copy of the 17 million pages of documents involved in this case.

Remember, this cost award was for vendor expenses only—namely vendor costs to process, store, and host the ESI. It did not include the attorney fees incurred to review these 17 million pages of documents from 2.7 million documents. We do not have a breakdown of the total fee award of $9,249,219.85 to determine how much of that expense was related to e-discovery. However, we do know that the total included work by both law firm attorneys and contract lawyers.

[3]No. 3:05-CV-0627-L, 2013 U.S. Dist. LEXIS 46529 (N.D. Tex. Mar. 31, 2013).

ATTACK ON CONTRACT LAWYERS' AWARD

The $9,249,219.85 fee award to the prevailing defendant included costs incurred for contract lawyer document review work. This was the correct procedure. It should not have been included on the cost side. Even though the contract lawyers may have been billed by an outside vendor, separate from the law firms representing the defendant, these expenses should not be included in a costs award. They are fees for legal services, regardless of the fact that the billings may have arisen from a nonlaw firm. The law and ethics require that their services be performed under the direct supervision of the law firms that were attorneys of record. Thus, contract lawyer fees should never be awarded as a cost, only as an attorney fee.

What contract lawyers do is legal work and legal services, even if much of it is hopelessly old-school and out of date. Anyone making decisions on the relevance of a document to a lawsuit (much less on issues, privilege, or confidentiality) is making a legal decision. They are providing a legal opinion and rendering a legal service. You have to be a licensed lawyer to do these things. It is not just a technicality, as I have heard some people say. These are core legal issues and it is a crime in most states for nonlawyers to engage in the unauthorized practice of law.

The plaintiff here attacked the reasonability of the fee award as it pertained to the contract lawyers by challenging the effectiveness of the contract lawyers' services. They alleged that their review was filled with errors and so not even worth the $85 per hour rate charged. The plaintiff only supported the alleged worthlessness with allegations that the defendant mistakenly produced many privileged documents. The effectiveness attack failed here, especially because the plaintiff also used contract lawyers, who also missed and produced some 23,000 privileged documents. Furthermore, the plaintiff's attack did not object to the whole mistaken notion of linear review, instead of more advanced analytics. Apparently all of that was beyond their grasp.

Here is Judge Whittemore's rejection of the argument made by the plaintiff in the instant case:

> Tampa Bay Water's expert opines that HDR's use of contract attorneys at a rate of $85.00 per hour was unnecessary and ineffective and that their fees should be reduced by 50 percent.

> Mr. Hill observed that contract attorneys were tasked with reviewing and coding documents (Dkt. 653-3, p. 35). This was confirmed by Mr. Mason, who averred that contract attorneys reviewed and coded the document productions for responsiveness and privilege (Dkt. 653-1, ¶ 13; Dkt. 672-1, p. 6, ¶ 15).
>
> Mr. Vento suggests that the fees incurred by contract attorneys were unreasonable because the contract attorneys made errors which resulted in the inadvertent disclosure of privileged documents. As HDR explained in its reply brief, the production of privileged documents was caused by a vendor computer error, not contract attorneys (Dkt. 672, p. 6). Further, given the 17 million pages of documents in this case, it is unrealistic to assume that there would be no inadvertent production of privileged documents. Indeed, it appears that Tampa Bay Water may have inadvertently produced some 23,000 privileged documents (Dkt. 316-12, Meaders Aff. ¶ 6).
>
> Mr. Vento also contends that contract attorneys performed work that was duplicative of outside vendors. But as Mr. Mason explained, outside vendors performed "objective coding," which involved reviewing documents and noting items such as the author, recipient, date, and document type. Internal teams, which included the contract attorneys, were tasked with "issue coding," which involved a more thorough review of the documents for privilege, responsiveness, and substantive issues. There was, therefore, no duplication in the coding process. To the extent Tampa Bay Water objects to the number of contract attorneys used by HDR, it misses the point. The review and coding of some 17 million pages of documents requires the same number of hours, whether the work is performed by one contract attorney or twenty-eight. While the contract attorneys' fees are not insubstantial, it was certainly reasonable for HDR to utilize these individuals to conduct an adequate review of the massive volume of documents, whether it was eight or eighteen.

Although the attack on contract lawyers for document review failed in this case, I think the basic idea of challenging the reasonability of contract lawyer fees based on their ineffectiveness could work in other cases. However, to do so, the losing party would first have to lay a proper predicate during the course of the case.

CONCLUSION

In a large case such as we see in *Tampa Bay Water v. HDR Engineering, Inc.* the expenditure of $3.1 million in e-discovery vendor costs alone was business as usual. Perhaps some money for vendors could have been saved in this case by using predictive coding, but perhaps not. The issue was never raised (although it is clear from my predictive coding experiments and experience, as well as many others, that attorney fees for review could certainly have been saved).

When using the old-style linear review, you can expect such million-dollar expenses as we see in *Tampa Bay Water,* even if this means that you must pay the vendor 10 percent of the case value. If you include the attorney fees for e-discovery, the total cost for old-time linear document review was probably more than 50 percent of the total cost of defense of the case. The court in this case had no problem finding such expenses to be reasonable. The prevailing defendant was awarded over $20 million in fees and costs to defend a $30 million case.

There are a couple of obvious lessons here. First of all, do not second-guess your mediation representatives and back out of a done deal at mediation. Second, never think you have the jury in the bag and cannot lose if you can just get the case to a jury. No reputable lawyer would ever tell you that. Tampa Bay Water thought that, and they lost $50 million so fast their heads were spinning. Third, make sure you have contracts that include prevailing party fees and cost awards; if you must sue someone, sue under these contracts. Do not bet upon liberal construction of the federal costs statute (28 USC §1920) to make you whole.

Finally, this opinion shows once again that linear review, even with contract lawyers, is very expensive. I personally do not think $0.18 per page is a great deal for 17 million pages. Plus, if you break it down by document (2.7 million files), which the order did not do, that is $1.15 per document. Again, remember that this is just the charge for processing and hosting the files. We can only guess what the total charge was per page, or per file, after the inclusion of attorney fees to actually review the files. If you assume an industry standard linear review speed of 50 files per hour by contract lawyers billing at $85 per hour, then it would take 54,000 hours to review all 2.7 million files. The total cost would be $4,590,000, which equals $1.70 per file. (Remember, the total fee award for this case was $9,249,219.85, so this $4.6 million estimate for review does not seem too out of line.) Thus, the total cost of review, both fees and costs, would be $2.85 per file.

The takeaway here is to both look for high-tech alternatives for your own review and, like the plaintiffs did in *Kleen Products*, suggest strongly that the other side do too.[4] That can give you a position to attack the reasonability of the other side's bloated attorney fee award request for document review. If you do not, and if you lose the case, you could end up paying for the other side's inefficient, bloated review, just like Tampa Bay Water did. Then, as a losing litigant in a contract dispute, you can end up being hit twice in the pocketbook—once by your own lawyers for their old-timey, bloated review, and then again for the other side's inefficiency. Sure, all of the lawyers win by that arrangement (which is why many wish I would just shut up) and some of the vendors do too, but for how long? Eventually, even the most loyal and trusting clients will catch on and move on.[5] The use of proper predictive coding search techniques is imperative in today's age of too much information.

---

[4]Kleen Products, LLC, et al. v. Packaging Corp. of Amer., et al., 10 C 5711 (N.D. Ill. Sept. 28, 2012).

[5]*See* Nicholas M. Pace & Laura Zakaras, *Where the Money Goes: Understanding Litigant Expenditures for Producing Electronic Discovery* (Rand Corporation 2012).

Party Ordered to Disclose Where and How It Searched for ESI: You Can Expect This Kind of Order to Become Commonplace

14

A federal court in Nebraska ordered a defendant to disclose all of the sources it searched to respond to an e-discovery request, as well as all of the keywords it used to perform its searches.[1] This order requiring the disclosure of keywords continues a legal trend.[2] The court in *American Home* did so in a somewhat unusual and instructive context that will be discussed in this chapter. Note that the plaintiff in *American Home* continued in its winning ways at trial and received a $9 million jury award, which was recently affirmed on appeal.[3]

The requesting party plaintiffs in the instant case filed a motion to compel production based solely on the fact that they expected to receive a larger production than they did. They did not point to any missing

---

[1] American Home Assurance Company et al. v. Greater Omaha Packing Company, Inc., No. 8:11CV270 (D. Neb. Sept. 11, 2013).
[2] *See* Formfactor, Inc. v. Micro-Probe, Inc., Case No. C-10-03095 PJH (JCS), 2012 WL 1575093, at *7 n.4 (N.D. Cal. May 3, 2012); Romero v. Allstate Ins. Co., 271 F.R.D. 96, 109-10 (E.D. Pa. 2010).
[3] American Home Assurance Co. v. Greater Omaha Packing Co., No. 15-1313 (8th Cir. 2016).

documents or even any types of documents that they expected to receive but did not. They just pointed to the size of the production—only 25 e-mails—and said that in itself provided good cause to order the defendant to produce more e-mails and other electronically stored information.

THE COURT'S RULING

Senior U.S. District Court Judge Lyle E. Strom denied the motion to compel production holding:

> [Plaintiff] has failed to identify a specific e-mail or electronic record that GOPAC is refusing to produce. Rather, Cargill argues that the small number of e-mails produced (25) evidences a lack of diligence in production. GOPAC has an obligation to promptly produce information resulting from timely searches of all digital records over which it has possession or control. However, the Court cannot compel the production of information that does not exist. GOPAC argued before the Court that prior to 2011, it had no central server on which e-mails were stored. GOPAC has further assured the Court that it has turned over all ESI that its searches produced and continues to supplement as it finds additional information. GOPAC has also offered to search available sources using search terms provided by Cargill, but Cargill has refused to supply any additional terms.

Still, Judge Strom went on to compel disclosure of defendant's search methods and sources as follows:

> To provide Cargill an adequate opportunity to contest discovery of ESI, the Court will order GOPAC to disclose the sources it has searched or intends to search and, for each source, the search terms used. The Court will also order all ESI based on the current search terms be produced by November 1, 2013. However, given Cargill's failure to point to any specific information that has been withheld or additional sources that have not been searched, no further action by the Court is appropriate at this time.

LESSONS LEARNED

Sometimes there simply is no, or very little, relevant evidence to be found. This is not surprising if a claim lacks a solid factual foundation. We all know that many frivolous claims are filed every day. For instance, if a request seeks production of all e-mails about employees that mention their race but no such e-mails exist, the proper response is that there are no documents responsive to the request. This fact alone should rarely trigger an order to compel. The responding party has already stated there is nothing to compel—that no such e-mails exist.

Still, more and more courts are requiring the responding party to go the extra step and disclose what searches they did before they concluded that no responsive documents existed. Do not expect that these efforts will always be protected by attorney work-product confidentiality. Expect instead that you will be asked to disclose your search efforts.[4] Always take care to be reasonable and diligent in your search for responsive evidence. You have a professional duty to do so, both under our ethics code and the rules of procedure.[5]

Also be prepared to disclose your diligence, which meant disclosure of keywords used and custodians searched in the Nebraska case. In other cases involving more sophisticated document review projects and multiple modes of search, it may involve more detailed disclosures than just keywords (e.g., disclosing what other search methods were used in addition to keywords).

Although we are not there yet, the day will surely come when use of only one search method—no matter what it is, but especially if it is as simplistic as linear review or keyword search—will be considered *per se* unreasonable.

---

[4]Apple Inc. v. Samsung Electronics Co. Ltd., No. 12-CV-0630-LHK (PSG), 2013 U.S. Dist. LEXIS 67085 (N.D. Cal. May 9, 2013); Formfactor, Inc. v. Micro-Probe, Inc., Case No. C-10-03095 PJH (JCS), 2012 WL 1575093, at *7 n.4 (N.D. Cal. May 3, 2012); Romero v. Allstate Ins. Co., 271 F.R.D. 96, 109-10 (E.D. Pa. 2010).

[5]*See, e.g.*, Rule 26(g).

LEARNED HAND

Is it really diligent to just plug in a few keywords and call that a search? In the 1990s, I would have said yes, certainly. In the early 2000s, I would have said yes, probably. In the second decade of the 21st century, I don't know. It depends. I am reminded again of the most famous tugboat in legal history, the *T.J. Hooper*, and its missing radio.[6]

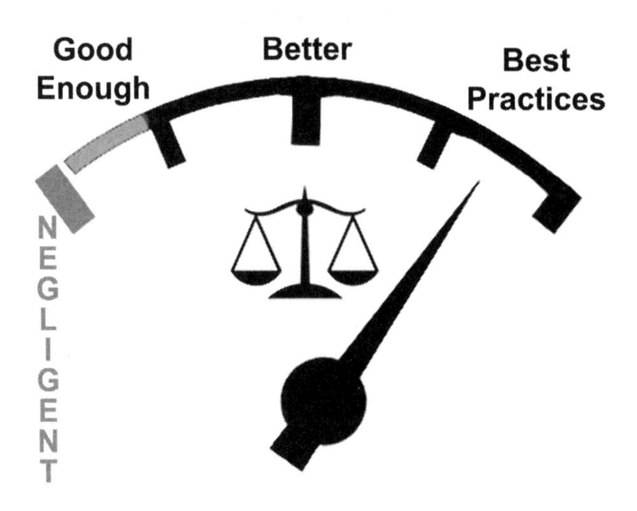

If the requesting party is ok with just doing a keyword search or even requests it, then the search may be fine. When, as in the *American Home* case, the requesting party declines to tell the responding party what to do and declines to buy into a keyword approach, then the acceptability of the search depends on a few factors. What keywords were used? How were they used? How much time and effort was spent on the search? Were the keywords tested? Were they adjusted and refined with sampling? Were Boolean connectors used? Were the keywords used parametrically, by which I mean in various metadata fields? Who did the searches? What were their qualifications? What other

[6]The T.J. Hooper v. Northern Barge Corp., 60 F.2d 737 (2d Cir. 1932) ("in most cases reasonable prudence is in fact common prudence; but strictly it is never its measure; a whole calling may have unduly lagged in the adoption of new and available devices.") (J. Learned Hand).

modes of search were used, and was there disclosure on each? What data were searched? Was it just one custodian or 10? Were all of their writings searched or just e-mail?[7]

The day will come when, unless stipulated to, the mere use of keyword search and neglect of all other types of search will not be good enough. The day will come when a judge finds that kind of search to be negligent and unreasonable, and thus orders a redo or imposes sanctions. It may even result in a judgment for malpractice. The day will come when a judge as brilliant and bold as Learned Hand finds that our whole profession has *unduly lagged in the adoption of new and available devices,* just like Judge Hand held that the entire shipping industry unduly lagged in using radios to monitor the weather. The learned judge will hold that the mere use of keywords alone, even though a professional norm of the legal industry, is still negligent. When that day comes, I want to be on the side moving for sanctions, not defending.

CONCLUSION

History is on the side of technology. Even if our legal profession is notoriously slow to adopt new technologies and new modes of search, you cannot fight the tide of history—just ask the buggy whip manufacturers. Although certain well-known and powerful bar groups may still teach tape dictation as part of their continuing legal education program—and not even mention predictive coding (I kid you not, I was there)—they are hopelessly out of date and walking anachronisms. They are teaching lawyers to use buggy whips. The future of our profession belongs to the technology minded—to those open to the adoption of new and available devices. Remember the lessons of negligence from Judge Learned Hand. Remember the *T.J. Hooper.*

---

[7]*See, e.g.,* United States v. O'Keefe, 537 F.Supp.2d 14, 24 (D.D.C. 2008) (J. Facciola) ("Whether search terms or "keywords" will yield the information sought is a complicated question involving the interplay, at least, of the sciences of computer technology, statistics and linguistics. Given this complexity, for lawyers and judges to dare opine that a certain search term or terms would be more likely to produce information than the terms that were used is truly to go where angels fear to tread.").

15 The Ethics of e-Discovery

I have been interested in the ethical issues surrounding electronic discovery since 2006. At that time, I phased out my general trial practice, started working full-time on e-discovery, joined the Sedona Conference, and started the e-Discovery Team blog. As part of my newly refocused practice, I started reading almost all of the opinions around the country written on e-discovery. I quickly noticed something I had not seen before in any other field of law. The case law was dominated by sanctions cases involving spoliation of evidence. (It still is.) Not only that, attorneys are often directly implicated in this spoliation and accused of many other types of intentional or negligent misconduct. I began to wonder back then if I had stepped into a crazy zone of the law where all attorneys acted like sharks. At this point, I am quite sure of that! After 10 years of observation, I have a pretty good understanding of what is going on and have constructed several nearly invulnerable shark cages.

This suspicion back in 2006 led me to think, write, and speak often on the subject of e-discovery ethics. That initially culminated in an article, *Lawyers Behaving Badly: Understanding Unprofessional Conduct in e-Discovery*.[1] The article led to my participation in a full-day academic seminar on the subject at Mercer Law School with noted e-discovery experts Judge John Facciola, Judge David Baker, Jason R. Baron, William Hamilton, Professor Monroe Freedman, and Chilton Varner.[2]

During that event, I came to understand that I had not wandered into a special zone of hell by specializing in e-discovery. Lawyers doing e-discovery were no worse, or no better, than other lawyers. However, they were put to special challenges and conditions unique to this new field of law. The end result was many more errors in judgment than you can find anywhere else. These errors continue, as shown by surveys of case law.[3]

LAWYERS BEHAVING BADLY

In my 2009 law review article, *Lawyers Behaving Badly*, I concluded that:

> [T]he profession has not suddenly become more sinister than before. Although, some suggest that the dominance of large firms as mega-business enterprises is causing a significant decline in overall ethics. *See* Marc Galanter & William Henderson, *The Elastic Tournament: A Second Transformation of the Big Law Firm,* 60 STAN. L. REV. 1867 (2008). There may be some truth to this, but a general decline in ethical standards does not explain why e-discovery jurisprudence is so rife with malfeasance.[4]

Instead, I hypothesized four reasons to explain the apparent frequent bad behavior of so many attorneys in the field of electronic discovery:

> There are four fundamental forces at work in e-discovery, which when considered together, explain most attorney misconduct:

---

[1] 60 MERCER L. REV. 983 (Spring 2009).
[2] The transcript of this event is published at 60 MERCER L. REV. 863 (Spring 2009).
[3] *See, e.g.*, Willoughby, Jones & Antine, *Sanctions for E-Discovery Violations: By the Numbers,* 60 DUKE L.J. 789 (2010).
[4] *Lawyers Behaving Badly, supra* at 985.

(1) a general lack of technological sophistication,
(2) over-zealous attorney conduct,
(3) a lack of development of professional duties as an advocate, and
(4) legal incompetence.

These "wicked quadrants" are depicted in the circular diagram shown here. I am not going to explore the ins and outs of the wicked quadrants in this chapter, nor rehash the reasons so many lawyers fall astray in e-discovery. (Interested readers are directed to the article and symposium transcript.) Instead, in this chapter, I will review and briefly analyze the primary rules of professional conduct that are implicated in e-discovery ethics. These are the rules that we should understand and rely upon to keep us on the straight and narrow and out of the sanctions penalty box. I will also present a common hypothetical scenario where the ethics of many lawyers involved in e-discovery productions are severely tested. Then, I will analyze the hypothetical scenario and show how these rules of professional conduct should apply.

ABA'S MODEL RULES OF PROFESSIONAL CONDUCT

The ethical codes require all lawyers to be competent, and, if faced with a legal task wherein they are not competent, such as e-discovery, to bring in other attorneys who are.

> **Rule 1.1**: A lawyer shall provide competent representation to a client. Competent representation requires the legal knowledge, skill, thoroughness, and preparation reasonably necessary for the representation.

Our ethics also require diligence—a task that is impossible unless you are competent and actually know what to do and when to do it.

> **Rule 1.3**: A lawyer shall act with reasonable diligence and promptness in representing a client.

Fast and efficient action is built into our code. It is emphasized again by requiring lawyers to expedite litigation:

> **Rule 3.2:** A lawyer shall make reasonable efforts to expedite litigation consistent with the interests of the client.

The duty of confidentiality is also a core value that often comes into play in e-discovery practice:

> **Rule 1.6:** A lawyer shall not reveal information relating to the representation of a client unless the client gives informed consent, the disclosure is impliedly authorized in order to carry out the representation or the disclosure is permitted by paragraph (b).

Our fundamental values embodied by our rules of professional conduct also require candor toward the tribunal—the judges. Candor means openness and complete honesty. It is a core value that may never be broken under any circumstances. Should it violate your duty of loyalty to your client, you are required to withdraw from representation rather than ever be dishonest and closed to the presiding judge. Here are the exact words of this most important of rules, **Rule 3.3**:

> (a) A lawyer shall not knowingly:
>
> (1) make a false statement of fact or law to a tribunal or fail to correct a false statement of material fact or law previously made to the tribunal by the lawyer; ...
>
> (3) offer evidence that the lawyer knows to be false....

Our core values as lawyers also require fairness to the opposing party in litigation and fairness to the opposing counsel. This means, among other things, that games of hide-the-ball are forbidden. This does not mean that you should provide evidence harmful to your client that was not requested, or not relevant, or that you are not legally required to produce such as privileged information. However, if it was requested, is relevant, and you are legally required to produce it, it is unethical not to do so. If the client refuses to do so, you should withdraw. **Rule 3.4** states in part:

> A lawyer shall not:
>
> (a) unlawfully obstruct another party's access to evidence or otherwise unlawfully alter, destroy, or conceal a document or other material having potential evidentiary value. A lawyer shall not counsel or assist another person to do any such act;
> (b) falsify evidence, counsel or assist a witness to testify falsely, or offer an inducement to a witness that is prohibited by law;
> (c) knowingly disobey an obligation under the rules of a tribunal, except for an open refusal based on an assertion that no valid obligation exists;
> (d) in pretrial procedure, make a frivolous discovery request or fail to make reasonably diligent effort to comply with a legally proper discovery request by an opposing party.

This last point in subsection (d) of Rule 3.4 is specifically directed to discovery requests and will be closely examined in our concluding hypothetical scenario.

BRIEF ANALYSIS OF THE RULES

To summarize our review of the ABA Model Rules of Professional Conduct, six rules seem especially important to the field of e-discovery:

- Rule 1.1—Competence
- Rule 1.3—Diligence
- Rule 1.6—Confidentiality
- Rule 3.2—Expediting Litigation

- Rule 3.3—Candor Toward the Tribunal
- Rule 3.4—Fairness to Opposing Party and Counsel

Rules 1.3 and 1.6, diligence and confidentiality, are often considered client-related duties, whereas the other rules listed above are considered professional duties. I examined the inherent tension between these rules in *Lawyers Behaving Badly,* which I illustrated with several diagrams.

My article suggests that many lawyers neglect their professional duties and overinflate client duties, instead of crafting a careful balance. I speculate that one reason for this imbalance is that the discharge of client-centric duties tends to receive immediate financial rewards from appreciative, perhaps overimpressed, clients. On the other hand, the reputation gains and societal values from fulfillment of professional duties are more longterm and abstract. In the hope that a picture actually may be worth a thousand words, and so spare you unnecessary reading at this time, I provide some diagram here. I suggest you seek the original article for a full explanation should your curiosity be stimulated.

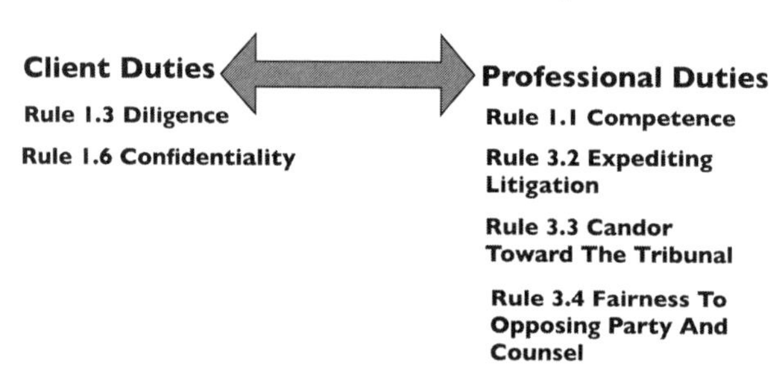

Attorney competence, Rule 1.1, is such a powerful force in our legal tradition that it is an oversimplification to look solely at the problem of ethics in e-discovery in a dualistic manner—client versus profession—as the above diagram suggests. Another element of complexity must be added to get a better understanding of the problem. *Competence* should be understood as its own ethical force, and the issue should be triangulated as shown here.

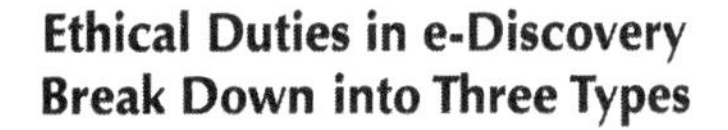

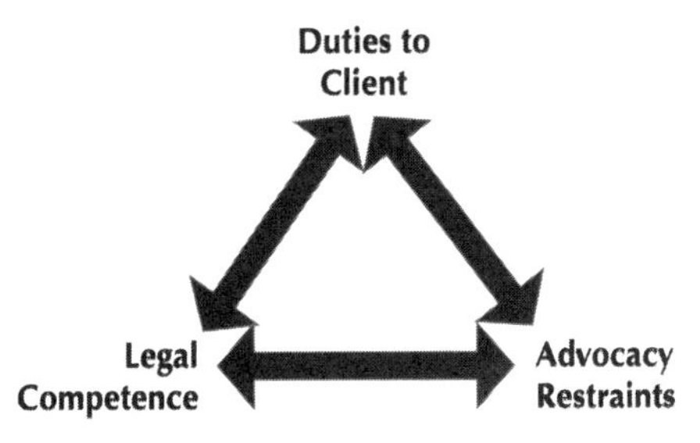

This threefold structural analysis allows for a deeper understanding of the true dynamics of legal practice. Legal competence serves as an independent upward force, along with professional duties, to counterbalance the pressures and temptations involved with fulfillment of duties to clients. The forces of law and profession work hand-in-hand to offset the demands of some clients, typically implied, to prevail over their adversaries at all costs.

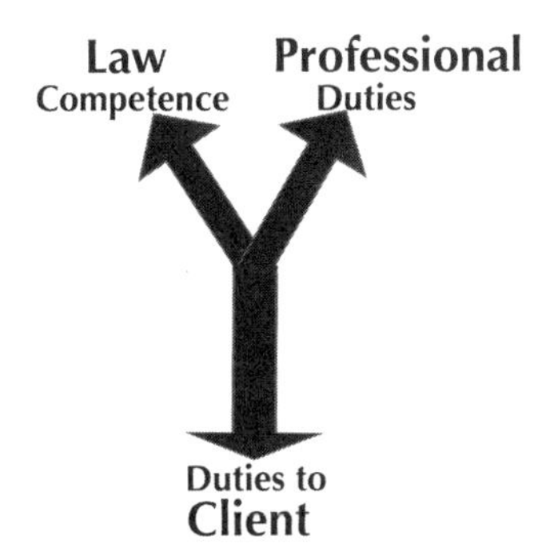

Most of the time, the temptations of greed and power do not cause lawyers to behave badly. Certainly, lawyers do not make a practice of lying to courts and opposing counsel, even though they could probably get away with it in many instances and maximize their income in the process. There is more to this picture than simple economics. The law, after all, attracts many who are concerned with justice and care about doing the right thing. Most lawyers have strong moral fiber and need little encouragement to do the right thing. They are more than pen-and-quill mercenaries—or, better put in today's world, more than digital warriors. Integrity, professional pride, and competence temper their financial motivations. Moreover, some enlightened clients recognize and financially reward professional competence and are influenced by professional reputation in the lawyer selection and compensation processes.

COOPERATION

The strategy demanded in e-discovery, when it is performed competently, is fundamentally different than traditional adversarial strategy for courtroom arguments. It involves cooperation on discovery, buttressed by liberal disclosure by both sides (a party requesting information and a party responding to the discovery requests). The need for this new strategy—and the name given therefore of *cooperation*—was initiated by Richard Braman, the late founder of the Sedona Conference. Richard set forth this Sedona initiative in a press conference followed by the *Sedona Conference Cooperation Proclamation* (2008). This brief document (2.5 pages) is well summarized by its conclusion, which states:

> It is time to build upon modern Rules amendments, state and federal, which address e-discovery. Using this springboard, the legal profession can engage in a comprehensive effort to promote pre-trial discovery cooperation. Our "officer of the court" duties demand no less. This project is not utopian; rather, it is a tailored effort to effectuate the mandate of court rules calling for a "just, speedy, and inexpensive determination of every action" and the fundamental ethical principles governing our profession.

Although the proclamation is short, it is elaborated at length in *The Case for Cooperation*,[5] which was written by a group of Sedona contributors led by Bill Butterfield of Hausfeld LLP. The executive editors were Richard G. Braman and Kenneth J. Withers, both of the Sedona Conference. This initial proclamation and article were followed by case law where all of the leading e-discovery judges weighed in

[5] 10 SEDONA CONF. J. 339 (2009 Supp.)

with their strong support of the new doctrine, as well as many more articles.[6]

The *cooperation challenge* is still beyond the skill of most attorneys, at least when it comes to making e-discovery-related decisions and communications. The competence weakness in turn limits the restraints on unethical conduct. The hardest ethical decisions have to be made where you are not sure what to do. As practitioners of e-discovery improve their technical competence, they realize that the cooperative model must be employed to focus on the issues and to control costs. I have yet to meet an experienced attorney in this field—one who knows both discovery and trial practice—who does not agree with this proposition.

HYPOTHETICAL SCENARIO

Let us assume for purposes of this hypothetical scenario that the attorneys for one side—the defendant employer in a class action case—have shifted to the new paradigm of cooperation; the attorneys for the other side—here the plaintiffs' counsel—have not. The plaintiffs' counsel are still stuck in the old-school attitude of attacking all of the other side's proposals without first considering their merits, without any objective analysis of reasonability. (I have seen this "hypothetical" happen many times.)

Attorneys do this because they assume that if the other side wants something, then it must be bad for their side. They assume that any

---

[6]Mancia v. Mayflower Textile Services Co. 253 F.R.D. 354 (D.Md. Oct. 15, 2008) (landmark case on cooperation by Judge Paul Grimm that details the basis in the rules and reasonable, ethical practice for a cooperative approach to discovery, especially e-discovery); Ralph Losey, *Mancia v. Mayflower Begins a Pilgrimage to the New World of Cooperation,* 10 SEDONA CONF. J. 377 (2009 Supp.) (reviews initial case law adopting the Cooperation Proclamation); S. Gensler, *The Bull's-Eye View of Cooperation in Discovery,* 10 SEDONA CONF. J. 363 (2009 Supp.) (Professor Gensler provides a scholarly basis and analysis of the new doctrine and its benefits to litigants). *Also see* DeGeer v. Gillis, 2010 WL 5096563 (N.D. Ill. Dec. 8, 2010) (J. Nolan) (found that the absence of a "spirit of cooperation [and] efficiency" was the controlling factor in determining whether cost shifting was warranted for discovery of nonparty ESI).

proposal is not genuine, that it is instead a gross exaggeration of the other side's real position. They assume anti-Solomon attitudes where the baby will be split. They do not cooperate. They negotiate. They want to win, and most will do so at all costs without regard to the unnecessary attorney fees thereby incurred.

Unfortunately, in e-discovery most attorneys are still stuck in the noncooperative win/lose discovery battle. They mistakenly think that it is their job to not only argue the law and apply the law to the given facts, but also to try to change the given facts and hide or obfuscate facts they think are adverse to their clients. This fundamental difference in attitude toward discovery makes the position of the *cooperator*, here defense counsel, very difficult. The solution is largely one of education of opposing counsel or, failing that, the court.

An objective reasonable discussion should resolve all issues, especially if there is a fair measure of transparency to the process. This must remain the goal of all cooperative counsel in order to protect their clients from excessive costs and disputes.

Next, assume that the plaintiffs' counsel makes a very broad demand for production of e-mail using the old-school, win-lose negotiation methods. Assume that they make demands for the relevant e-mails from 50 custodians, naming everyone and their uncle who might possibly have anything to do with the dispute in question. They also purport to define relevancy very broadly by making 50 category demands on a wide variety of subjects, many with only a nebulous connection to the factual issues of the case. They do so knowing that at most 10 custodians are likely to really know anything, but they are not sure exactly who they are; for that reason, they name the larger group of 50. They are also not sure of the real issues of fact in the case yet, largely because they have never talked with opposing counsel. Because they do not have a clear idea of the issues in the case, they define relevancy very broadly with 50 categories of documents.

The new paradigm attorneys—here defense counsel—quickly realize when they attempt real communication with the plaintiffs' counsel on issues of e-discovery, they are dealing with old-school negotiators. It quickly becomes obvious to experienced e-discovery counsel when opposing counsel has little or no personal competence in the area. You cannot hide that, no matter how many experts you may hire to guide you.

Defense counsel quickly realizes that no true communications are likely and that they are engaged in a traditional negotiation process with the plaintiffs' counsel. But rather than accept and play the game (say, by offering three custodians and five issues, hoping to settle for five custodians and seven issues), defense counsel lays out their case for five custodians and seven issues. They play a new game—a cooperative game of reasoned discussion and informed decisions. Defense counsel makes disclosure and explains why they consider the 5/7 offer to be reasonable. They explain why they think the offer would be beneficial to all parties.

Next, assume that the plaintiffs' counsel are not persuaded by defense counsel, respond with little or no substance, and instead demand 30/30 (30 custodians and 30 categories) instead of their initial 50/50. They argue that they have now made major concessions, thus suggesting or signaling that they will accept 20 custodians and 20 issues. They assume, incorrectly, that defense counsel is like them—that the 5/7 proposal was just the opening offer in a negotiation dance. They do not really care about the reasons stated by the defendants for the proposal, and, truth be told, they do not really understand most of the e-discovery technical talk surrounding the issues. They are hardball trial lawyers—tough advocates doing their job by pounding out as much information from the other side as they can. They think it would help their clients to make the defendants' case as expensive as possible. They know e-discovery is a good way to do that and they know from past experience that this *oppose everything* tactic is a good way to drive up the settlement value of the case. Discovery, especially e-discovery, is just another tool in the battle against the other side.

Next, assume that the defendants continue to refuse to play the negotiation game; hearing no real reasons for them to think their original calculation of five custodians and seven issues is wrong, they press forward in their demands for 5/7. They ask for reasons and calm discussion from the plaintiffs' counsel but instead receive rhetoric and negotiation bluster. Accusatory letters are exchanged—the real purpose of which are not true communications, but mere posturing and mere creation of exhibits for use in motion practice.

The court is then asked to consider cross-motions for relief on a variety of complex e-discovery issues. Both sides claim that they are the true cooperator and that the opposing party, not them, is to blame for the impasse. What should a judge do? How do you tell the true cooperator from the mere poser? Both sides claim to be cooperators, and one side *does* make a major move in custodian and issue count, whereas the other does not. From the negotiation perspective, it looks like the plaintiffs' counsel is being more cooperative. We know that they are not cooperating at all; they are not even communicating or attempting to narrow the issues. How is a savvy judge to sort things out?

The answer lies in probing the merits of the dispute. This requires the judge to also break out of the old negotiation paradigm and look beyond the numbers on the surface. Why are 5 custodians reasonable and proportional but 20 custodians too much? Why should relevancy be defined by 7 issues, not 20? It is not a mere numbers game, as the plaintiffs' counsel in this scenario would suggest. The court must do the hard work of examining the merits of the dispute—of determining what is reasonable and proportional for the case and what is not. The court should refuse to buy into the old paradigm negotiation model, which would just split the difference and enter an order allowing 12 custodians and 14 issues. The judge should instead examine the facts in an objective manner; if 5 custodians and 7 issues are indeed reasonable, then the judge should rule accordingly. This takes time and hard work on the judge's part, as well as on the part of the attorneys who frame the issues and present the case. They need to provide meat for the bone. They need to make disclosures and present facts to support their positions.

Let us further assume that defense counsel realized their quandary and voluntarily made substantial disclosures. Assume that they disclosed their own mental impressions as to why the five custodians they picked would have the most relevant e-mail. Assume they also provided total counts and other metrics of e-mail for the five custodians they proposed. Moreover, assume the defendant also provided counts for the additional 15 custodians that the plaintiffs' proposed.

Assume that the defendants made even more disclosures to support their argument of reasonability and proportionality under Rule 26(b)(1). Assume they presented detailed information concerning the costs of the review and production proposed by plaintiffs, as compared to their proposal. Assume it was not puffed or inflated and was supported by facts, which they offered to back up with further testimony if needed.

Assume that the defendants went even further and began to make sample productions from the top five custodians they picked, and that they did so after a strong confidentiality and Rule 502(d) clawback order was entered by the court. Assume the e-mails produced showed that most of the other 15 custodians that the plaintiffs wanted to add at great additional cost were copied on most of the relevant documents.

Assume that defense counsel even made some random sample productions from all 20 custodians to show that the top five they had selected had the vast majority of the relevant documents and were the only source of the few highly relevant documents found. Assume they not only produced the documents they marked relevant but also made a selective disclosure of documents (nonconfidential documents) they marked irrelevant to provide the plaintiffs with an opportunity to review and, if need be, to challenge their understanding of relevancy in this case.

Assume that the defense counsel was also proposing phased production. They only insisted their 5/7 approach be for the first phase; they did not insist that the plaintiffs waive their rights to seek additional document productions in follow-up phases. Instead, assume the defendants only sought to clarify that they reserved their rights to object to any future discovery, depending on the circumstances.

With all of these additional facts and voluntary disclosures, the judge's work becomes much easier. The judge now has the information on which to make a ruling under Rule 26(b)(1). The defendant has made significant disclosures of their client's e-mail systems and even of their e-mail contents. Now, the judge is in a position to determine whose position is reasonable and who the true cooperator is here. This information provides the substance needed for the judge to go beyond the negotiation model of discovery dispute resolution to a true judicial model.

Of course, in the real world, all lawyers come before judges with a history. They have a reputation. The importance of this cannot be overstated. This can also help a judge to evaluate who is a poser and who is not. This is especially true where a judge has seen and heard from one or more of the lawyers several times before. That is where the intangible value of an attorney's reputation comes in.

In my experience, when most judges are faced with this situation and are properly advised of the issues, they will do the hard work and make their own determination of reasonability. They will not simply split the baby and order 12 custodians and 14 issues. However, this requires proper education of judges on the issues, which in turn requires competent counsel with a good reputation for truth, honesty, and fair dealing. If defense counsel in this scenario are competent and have a good reputation, a just and reasoned result will usually be attained, regardless of any overly clever negotiation tactics of the plaintiffs' counsel.

ETHICAL ANALYSIS OF THE HYPOTHETICAL

What ethical considerations and rules or professional conduct come into play in this scenario? Let us analyze the facts of the hypothetical one rule at a time and consider the impact of all six of the key rules: Rule 1.1—Competence, Rule 1.3—Diligence, Rule 1.6—Confidentiality, Rule 3.2—Expediting Litigation, Rule 3.3—Candor Toward the Tribunal, and Rule 3.4—Fairness to Opposing Party and Counsel.

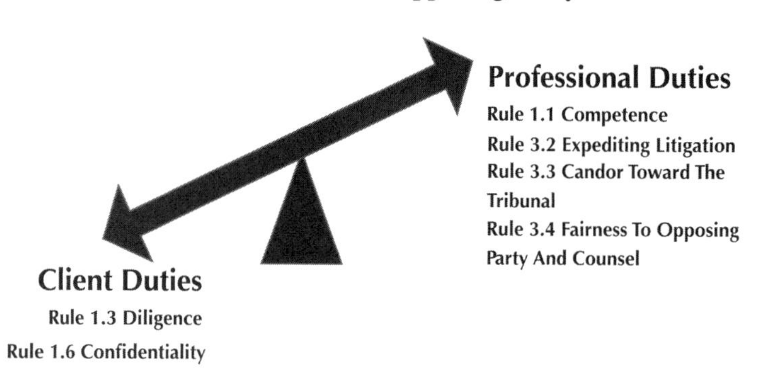

Competence

The competency issue here is critical, as it is in most ethical considerations. One party here, the plaintiffs' counsel, does not really understand e-discovery. For instance, they did not really understand many of the technical reasons behind the defendant's position, such as deduplication of e-mail copies throughout the system, nor the sampling disclosures. They did not understand the benefits of phased discovery and going first for the low-hanging fruit—the e-mails of the best key custodians.

They did not cooperate in e-discovery because they did not know how. They probably had never even seen the cooperative model in action before; therefore, when they saw it here, they did not recognize it. They may instead have mistaken it for weak or timid opposing counsel. It just provoked them to be more like cavemen. They got more aggressive in the face of the unknown. They also ran away from any real discussion on technical issues. This is a classic case of the fight-or-flight instincts of a non-computer-literate lawyer faced with e-discovery.

The plaintiffs' counsel in our hypothetical scenario did not trust the other side because they assumed the defendants were like them. They were not competent enough to recognize or understand the new approach. They only understood "cooperation" from the outside, as just another tool or keyword—a mere pretext in the game of hide-the-ball. They certainly had not read Professor Gensler's article and had no understanding at all on how the new cooperative, transnegotiation model might help their clients. In Professor Gensler's words:

> The Cooperation Proclamation is exactly right when it urges lawyers to see cooperation as a means for advancing their clients' interests and not as a retreat from their duties as loyal advocates. As I have written elsewhere, the lawyers who default to battle mode in discovery—who fail even to consider whether cooperation might yield better results—are the ones who truly fail to serve their clients' interests.[7]

They had also not read the article by the Sedona Conference making the legal case for cooperation.[8] The editor-in-chief of this article was the plaintiffs' well-known counsel, William P. Butterfield. The concluding paragraph of *The Case for Cooperation* succulently warns of what may happen to our system of justice if the new cooperative model to discovery is not adopted:

> If parties are expected to continue to manage discovery in the manner envisioned by the Federal Rules of Civil Procedure,

---

[7] *The Bull's-Eye View of Cooperation in Discovery*, 10 Sedona Conf. J. 363 (2009 Supp.).

[8] *The Case for Cooperation*, *supra*.

> cooperation will be necessary. Without such cooperation, discovery will become too expensive and time consuming for parties to effectively litigate their disputes.[9]

The plaintiffs' counsel here did not even seem to understand what most truly competent plaintiffs' counsel do—that every dollar spent on useless discovery is another dollar not available for settlement. The best, most competent counsel have always saved their powder for the real battles that count, on the law and application of the law to the facts. They have always understood that the true and only valid purpose of discovery is to get at the *key facts* to allow reasoned evaluation of the case, not to prepare mountains of data, extort the responding party, or bury the requesting party in a document dump. Competent legal counsel do not engage in *discovery as abuse*. Those that do soon develop a reputation that follows them into a courtroom, even on the other side of the country from where they usually practice.[10] As the Sedona Conference noted, the "risk of gaining a reputation among the judiciary as unduly combative during discovery, encourages cooperative behavior."[11]

The only possible conclusion here is that the plaintiffs were not competent enough to handle the e-discovery issues in this class-action employment case. For that reason alone, under this scenario they behaved unethically. They violated Rule 1.1.

Many attorneys in this situation attempt to meet their ethical obligation of competence by hiring an e-discovery vendor to advise them. Unfortunately, this usually does not work because such "experts" frequently only tell the attorneys who hired them what they want to hear. The hired guns simply supply arguments jazzed up with tech-speak to support the legal argument of the attorneys who hired them.

In any event, e-discovery vendors are technologists, not lawyers. Even when a rare e-discovery expert at a vendor also has a law degree, he or she is not allowed to provide legal advice. The only way that attorneys who are not competent in the law and the practice of e-discovery can fulfill their ethical duties is by taking the time and considerable efforts

---

[9] *Id.* at 362.
[10] *See Discovery as Abuse*, 69 B.U. L. Rev. 635 (1989).
[11] *The Case for Cooperation, supra* at 362.

needed to become competent or by bringing in legal counsel who is competent to assist them. Vendors cannot render legal advice—end of story.

Diligence

The plaintiffs' counsel here thought they were being diligent because they were engaging in what they saw as vigorous advocacy. However, they were playing the wrong game. True vigorous advocacy here would have entailed detailed examination of the reasons provided by defense counsel for the five custodians and seven issues. It would have required reciprocal disclosures on their part on their thinking and analysis of the importance of the various custodians to the case. Diligence would have required immediate study of the e-mails produced. It would have taken the dispute out of rhetoric and knee-jerk opposition to everything the other side proposes and into the facts and legal analysis. That is what diligent lawyers should do.

The plaintiffs' counsel in this scenario were not diligent at all. Their incompetence made that impossible. They thought they were being very diligent and no doubt so did their clients, who are usually very easily impressed by the kind of saber-rattling in which they engaged. However, they did all of the wrong things. They engaged in knee-jerk opposition to everything the other side proposed, and this pretend diligence was really not diligent at all. Discovery as abuse is not an exercise in competent diligence. It is abuse, pure and simple.

Confidentiality

The plaintiffs' counsel here thought they were being very ethical by refusing to disclose their work product. They would not give the defendant an idea on their thinking of the case or on what information they thought would be highly relevant. They would not disclose why they thought some custodians and issues were more important. That was their confidential thinking and they thought they should keep it secret. They hoped to keep their analysis of the case (assuming they had one and this was not just a superficial form-driven lawsuit) to themselves. They wanted to surprise the defendants as much as possible. Indeed, they were initially surprised by how much confidential information the defense counsel here provided, which, again, they mistakenly mistook as a sign of weakness and egged them on to keep demanding more and more. Then, they were surprised again when defense counsel said no and never budged from the initial 5/7. Finally, they were surprised by the court ruling against them.

Which attorneys in this scenario met their ethical duty under Rule 1.6 to "not reveal information relating to the representation of a client" and which did not? Rule 1.6 has numerous exceptions to the duty of client confidentiality, including where the client gives informed consent or the "disclosure is impliedly authorized in order to carry out the representation." Here, the disclosure by defense counsel was needed to carry out the representation and so was impliedly authorized, even if not specifically authorized. Note that under the scenario, no attorney-client privileged documents or any privileged communications are disclosed. Even client confidential documents are protected under a strong confidentiality order or are not disclosed at all, just summarized. Any nonrelevant documents produced would also be covered by the confidentiality order and would be promptly returned. Further protection was provided by a strong clawback order.

The only confidential information disclosed here is *some* of the work-product privileged thinking and analysis of defense counsel. Unlike the attorney-client privilege, which is held by the client and can only be released by the client, the work-product privilege is held by the *attorney* and released by the attorney. The disclosure of the attorney's work product was made here to advance their client's interests. It was made to facilitate efficient, cost-effective search and production, and later to obtain a protective order preventing unduly burdensome, disproportionate e-discovery. Under new Rule 26(b)(1), this disproportionate information is outside of the scope of relevant, discoverable information. This kind of disclosure does not violate defense counsel's duties under Rule 1.6.

My conclusion is based on an understanding of how a work-product privileged waiver is different from an attorney-client privileged waiver. It does not automatically open up the door for further inquiries as an attorney-client waiver might do:

> The work product doctrine protects both deliberative materials such as mental impressions, conclusions, opinions, and legal

theories and factual materials prepared in anticipation of litigation.... In his declaration in support of summary judgment, David Frohlich, an Assistant Director in the SEC's Division of Enforcement, explains that the handwritten notes sought by Plaintiff were generated during the Cendant investigation in anticipation of litigation with Mr. Corigliano, Mr. Kearney, and others. Plaintiff does not dispute this statement and concedes that these documents qualify as attorney work product. However, Plaintiff contends that the SEC has waived any work product privilege with respect to these documents because similar handwritten notes were disclosed to Plaintiff during the criminal prosecution of Mr. Forbes. According to the declaration of Christopher R. Hart, an attorney at Williams & Connolly LLP, at least eleven of the documents of handwritten notes identified in the Vaughn index were produced by the government during the Forbes matter. Plaintiff thus contends that the government has "waived the work product privilege as to entire subject matter of handwritten notes between SEC staff and Corigliano, Kearney, or their respective counsel."

As with the attorney-client privilege, a party may waive the work product privilege through disclosure. *See In re United Mine Workers of Am. Employee Benefit Plans Litig.*, 159 F.R.D. 307, 310 (D.D.C. 1994) ("It seems ... clear in this Circuit that the disclosure of documents protected by the attorney work product privilege waives the protections of the attorney work product privilege as to the documents disclosed."). **However, "the test for waiving attorney work product protection is more stringent than the test for waiving attorney-client privilege."** *Goodrich Corp. v. U.S. Envtl. Prot. Agency*, 593 F. Supp. 2d 184, 191 (D.D.C. 2009). Although disclosure of documents waives attorney-client privilege with respect to all other communications related to the same subject matter, **the scope of "subject matter waiver" with respect to work product materials is more limited. "[A] subject-matter waiver of the attorney work product privilege should only be found when it would be inconsistent with the purposes of the work**

product privilege to limit the waiver to the actual documents disclosed." "Several factors figure into the analysis: whether disclosure was intentional or inadvertent, the breadth of the waiver sought, and the extent to which the requested documents would reveal litigation strategies or trial preparations"[12] (emphasis added).

The law provides greater protection to a work-product waiver, so the disclosures made in the hypothetical should leave defense counsel protected from any further unwanted intrusions.[13]

As for the conduct of the plaintiffs' counsel, it may surprise you to know that I do not conclude they have violated Rule 1.6. I must conclude that the plaintiffs' stonewalling actions in this case are also consistent with Rule 1.6. Although their behavior in this hypothetical scenario was unethical under the other rules here considered, it was not under Rule 1.6. They have the right to keep all of their work-products to themselves, even though it was stupid to do so and thus a probable violation of Rule 1.1 on competence, but it was *their* work-product. Of course, no rule should be considered in isolation and work-product thinking is required to be disclosed under many rules of civil procedures, especially including Rule 26(f), and any time you are seeking relief from the court or making final preparation for trial, not to mention trial itself.

Craig Ball, an e-discovery expert and former plaintiff's counsel, had this to say in a private discussion group for law professors we both belong to concerning the policy behind limited work-product disclosures, starting with a comment on pre-digital paper productions:

> You may argue that we never got to look behind a lawyer's decisions to produce or withhold even if the lawyer made the selections by throwing documents down the stairs and producing only what hit the next landing. But perhaps that's not an

[12]*See* Williams & Connolly LLP v. U.S. Securities and Exchange Commission, 2010 U.S. Dist. LEXIS 78570 (D.D.C. Aug. 4, 2010.)

[13]*Also see* Rule 502 *Federal Rules of Evidence*, and note that our hypothetical assumes a strong confidentiality and clawback order under Rule 502(d).

> approach we want to replicate in post-digital practice. We indulged ourselves in the belief that, right or wrong, relevance and privilege determinations were a lawyer's to make and largely immune from being second-guessed absent evidence of gross dereliction or misconduct. But, as we move into the realm of search technology–and especially those like keyword search only lately appreciated to be deeply flawed–the tools and methods employed must be closely examined and tested, including by exposing them to adversarial challenge. Perhaps we need to step away from our reflexive "we are lawyers and we are special," in order to consider what approaches are calculated to best serve the ends of justice. Cooperation demands communication. If you believe the first is more than a pipe dream, you need to embrace the latter.

I have to agree with my old friend Craig on this one. Opposing counsel needs to talk with each other and explain what they are doing in the area of search and production. You do not have to give up all your trade secrets, nor reveal all of your strategies, but you have to be prepared to disclose enough to show your reasonable, good-faith efforts. What does cooperation look like? It looks like lawyers talking and making mutual disclosures needed to plan discovery in a case.

Expediting Litigation

The conduct of the plaintiffs' counsel here violated their duty to expedite litigation. They did so in spite of the fact that expedited litigation is almost always consistent with a plaintiff's interest in a civil proceeding for a speedy trial. The plaintiffs' counsel here unethically violated this duty to expedite by forcing unnecessary motion practice. Furthermore, the closed approach of the plaintiffs' counsel to try to conceal the facts they really wanted in discovery probably also violated Rule 3.2, even if it did not violate Rule 1.6.[14]

---

[14] *See, e.g.,* DeGeer v. Gillis, 755 F. Supp. 2d 909, 930 (N.D. Ill. 2010) (if parties had participated in "candid, meaningful discussion of ESI at the outset of the case," expensive and time-consuming discovery and motions practice could have been avoided). *Also see* revised Rule 1, *FRCP.*

Candor Toward the Tribunal

I think the conduct of the plaintiffs' counsel in this hypothetical scenario violated the fundamental rule of professional conduct, but I admit that their violation might be seen as technical. This kind of conduct goes on every day in legal practice and is tolerated by both bench and bar. The plaintiffs' counsel here did not "make a false statement of fact or law to a tribunal … or, offer evidence that the lawyer knows to be false." However, they did not provide the whole truth either. They made a demand in their motion to compel for 30 custodians and 30 issues, and they continued in this demand at the hearing before the tribunal. Let us assume that they also made oral representations to the judge at a hearing that they thought this 30/30 demand was necessary and appropriate under the facts of the case and governing law. However, that is at best a half-truth because they had been willing all along to accept 20/20.

For that reason, they did not display the kind of candor to the tribunal that I personally think is appropriate. Instead, they continued to play the only game they knew how—the *negotiation game*—and they treated the judge as just another player in the game. In a negotiation game, you are never completely candid. That would defeat the whole point of the game. If the plaintiffs' counsel here were in fact candid to the tribunal, they would admit that 20/20 is their goal; however, that could be a slippery slope for them. It could also lead to the admission of their basic incompetence to do e-discovery to begin with, and might encourage them to engage in meaningful discussion and analysis, and enter into a true cooperative dialogue with the other side.

Fairness to Opposing Party and Counsel

Some attorneys are surprised when they see the terms of this important rule of professional conduct. Candor to the tribunal is one thing, but fairness to the opposing party and their attorneys is simply not part of the culture of many lawyers and law firms. They seem surprised when they are reminded that the requirement is built into our rules of ethics. It is not a mere professional courtesy, as some think—it is an ethical imperative. Under Rule 3.4, a lawyer shall not "unlawfully obstruct another party's access to evidence." A lawyer shall not "conceal a document or other material that the lawyer knows or reasonably should know is relevant to a pending or a reasonably foreseeable proceeding; nor counsel or assist another person to do any such act." A lawyer shall not "make a frivolous discovery request or fail to make reasonably diligent effort to comply with a legally proper discovery request by an opposing party."

The attorneys for the party responding to the discovery request in this hypothetical scenario, defense counsel, complied with their ethical duties. My conclusion assumes that they sought to limit discovery for the grounds stated, burdensomeness, and likely relevance. I assume they did not have any bad-faith ulterior motives, such as an attempt to conceal evidence that they knew to be unfavorable to their client. I assume they were not just trying to obstruct access to evidence or conceal relevant ESI. Finally, I assume that their search and production efforts were reasonably diligent.

With these assumptions, I conclude that defense counsel acted ethically because their refusal to review and produce any more than five custodians and seven issues in the first round of phased discovery did not prevent disclosure of any evidence they knew to be relevant, and it did not prevent the plaintiffs' later discovery from other custodians or issues that might prove necessary. It might delay it to a second phase, but not prevent it. If defense counsel should uncover a document outside of this scope, one that is obviously relevant, then under this rule they would be required to disclose such a document and should not conceal it.

I conclude to the contrary that, under the given facts, the plaintiffs' counsel violated the duty of fairness to opposing counsel because their initial request for discovery was frivolous. They signed and served a discovery request for 50 custodians and 50 issues, knowing that was excessive; for that reason, they quickly dropped to 30/30 and were ready to accept 20/20, which is what they really thought was reasonable all along. They used a request for production as a mere negotiation tool, and in so doing made an unethically frivolous discovery request. Note they also violated Rule 26(g) of the FRCP, which Judge Grimm in *Mancia* said was the most misunderstood and underutilized of all rules of procedure. Rule 26(g) is similar to Rule 11, but it applies only to the discovery pleadings. Rule 26(g)(1)(B) states that a signature on a discovery request constitutes an attorney's certification that the request is:

> (ii) not interposed for any improper purpose, such as to harass, cause unnecessary delay, or needlessly increase the cost of litigation; and...
>
> (iii) neither unreasonable nor unduly burdensome or expensive, considering the needs of the case, prior discovery in the case, the amount in controversy, and the importance of the issues at stake in the action.

The plaintiffs' counsel thought that 20 custodians and 20 issues was proportional, yet they signed a request for production seeking 50. They did so for purposes of setting up a negotiation. This is, I suggest, an improper purpose under Rule 26(g)(1)(B)(ii). They knew 50 was unreasonable and unduly burdensome, yet they still signed the discovery request. The plaintiffs' counsel in this hypothetical scenario thereby intentionally violated Rule 26(g)(1)(B)(iii), triggering a mandatory obligation under the rule for the court to impose sanctions.

This conduct by the requesting party was not only a civil rule violation—it was unethical. It violated professional rule of conduct 34(c) by "knowingly disobeying an obligation under the rules of a tribunal," namely Rule 26(g)(1)(B). Also, as explained before, it violated ethics Rule 3.4(d) because it was frivolous.

CONCLUSION

Some may say that my hypothetical scenario is far-fetched—that attorneys do not engage in this type of behavior. I say, "Get real." It is an everyday occurrence. The only thing far-fetched about it is the simplicity of the facts, which I necessarily injected into the hypothetical, and the relatively mild nature of the violations. In my position as national e-discovery counsel for an 800-plus attorney law firm with more than 50 offices around the country, I see equivalent or worse behavior by opposing counsel almost every week. It is not exactly a crazy hell-zone, as I used to suspect and many still believe.[15] However, it is bad, and we need to work together as a profession to break out of this prison.

Even though this hypothetical is an all-too-common scenario, as far as I know, no attorney has ever been reprimanded for an ethical violation of Rule 34 upon these circumstances. This ethics rule, like the 26(g) procedure rule, is a paper tiger. Indeed, you could say that about all of the ethics rules here discussed in the context of e-discovery. It is a new area of the law and state bar associations are naturally reluctant to enforce its rules in this virgin territory.

Still, just because attorneys are not yet being reprimanded or losing their licenses for these kinds of rule violations, we should still care about compliance. Following these well-established rules is the best way to stay on the straight and narrow when it comes to e-discovery. We cannot let old hide-the-ball practices morph into hide-the-byte operating systems.

Compliance with the rules of professional conduct and the new doctrine of cooperation that implements these rules (and the rules of civil procedure as Judge Grimm and Professor Gensler have pointed out) is the best way to avoid the threat warned of by Sedona and many others. It is the best way to avoid a future world of litigation where standard hide-the-byte operating systems make "discovery too expensive and time consuming for parties to effectively litigate their disputes."[16]

Although a good argument was made for the enactment of new rules of civil procedure to adapt to the challenges of e-discovery, new rules of professional conduct are not needed. The rules we have are sufficient to guide us, but we need to take the time and effort to study and understand them. We need to discuss these rules and how they apply to the new situations presented in e-discovery practice. It is my hope that this early effort in that direction will stimulate more discussion and analysis of the subject.

---

[15]Krueger v. Pelican Products Corp., C/A No. 87-2385-A (W.D. Okla. 1989) (J. Alley) ("If there is a hell to which disputatious, uncivil, vituperative lawyers go, let it be one in which the damned are eternally locked in discovery disputes with other lawyers of equally repugnant attributes.")
[16]*The Case for Cooperation*, *supra* at 362.

16 Judge David Waxse on Cooperation and Lawyers Who Act Like Spoiled Children

As discussed in the last chapter, a core problem facing the law today is the inability of lawyers to cooperate with each other. This failure is one of the primary causes of the explosive growth of e-discovery expense. It also explains the general lack of civility that now plagues our profession. Judge David J. Waxse added to the growing body of legal scholarship in this area with his excellent article, *Cooperation—What Is It and Why Do It?*[1] This chapter summarizes the article with the intent of enticing you to read the whole thing. You will also want to cite to this article in your legal practice, especially when dealing with lawyers who still play the old game of "fight everything." The article offers practical rule-based advice on how to deal with lawyers like this. Professor Gensler, whom Judge Waxse cites with approval, compares such lawyers to spoiled children.[2] This problem of petulant children in the law is very real, as I well know. If you are dealing with such counsel in any of your cases, I highly recommend that you read and use Judge Waxse's fine article.

---

[1] XVIII RICH. J. L. & TECH. 8 (2012).
[2] Steven S. Gensler, *Judicial Case Management: Caught in the Crossfire*, 60 DUKE L.J. 669, 734–37 (2010).

WHAT HAPPENS WHEN A PETULANT CHILD GETS A LICENSE TO PRACTICE LAW?

Professor Gensler, who has served on the Federal Rules Advisory Committee, picks up the spoiled child theme from another professor before him on the committee:

> Professor Thomas Rowe, himself a former member of the Advisory Committee, has observed that the case-management model will inevitably struggle to control costs if lawyers continue to act like spoiled children, requiring judges to provide the equivalent of constant adult supervision. Perhaps this suggests that what we need is not new rules but better play.[3]

Professor Gensler goes on to note that:

> Too often, lawyers simply default to battle mode in discovery, without even considering what they are fighting over, why they are fighting, or whether it is in their clients' best interests to fight over that particular item.…
>
> Cooperation skeptics, however, would argue that the cooperative ideal is unrealistic because lawyers and clients will continue to view it as advantageous to demand everything and produce little. If that is true, then we are effectively left, at best, with Professor Rowe's spoiled children in need of constant "adult supervision," and at worst with his "adversarial scorpions in [the] litigation bottle." In that event, the case-management model may well need to be paired with something else—perhaps significant structural reforms—if it is to succeed.[4]

I agree with the sentiments of the professors. So does Judge Waxse, who is famous for threatening to require lawyers to videotape their Rule 26(f) conferences. As Judge Waxse put it in his new article:

> Lawyers are more cooperative when they know that the judge is watching (providing "adult supervision") and enforcing cooperation responsibilities.[5]

---

[3] *Id.* at 734.
[4] *Id.* at 735, 738
[5] *Cooperation—What Is It and Why Do It?*, *supra* at 17.

Judge Waxse concludes this article by elaborating on the *spoiled child* theme:

> Finally, it may be helpful for a few lawyers to remind them that cooperation is something they should have learned in school. Some, who cannot seem to learn to cooperate, might benefit from this list for elementary school teachers, explaining how to be a cooperative person:
>
> > LISTEN carefully to others and be sure you understand what they are saying.
> >
> > SHARE when you have something that others would like to have.
> >
> > TAKE TURNS when there is something that nobody wants to do, or when more than one person wants to do the same thing.
> >
> > COMPROMISE when you have a serious conflict.
> >
> > DO YOUR PART the very best that you possibly can. This will inspire others to do the same.
> >
> > SHOW APPRECIATION to people for what they contribute.
> >
> > ENCOURAGE PEOPLE to do their best.[6]

This is good advice for persons of any age. You might think that lawyers do not need such simplistic advice. However, the state bars only test for intellectual comprehension, not maturity. Once a law school graduate is armed with a license to practice law, the petulant child types who never grew up can do a lot of damage to our system of justice. This is especially true if they are raised in a law firm culture that encourages *adversarial scorpion* tactics. Often, these firms look for and recruit overzealous types. They have ways to make them even more vicious and drunk with power.

Judge Waxse recognized the psychological dynamics at work here:

> [L]awyers who become litigators often have personalities that love conflict and competition. They do not enjoy cooperation

---

[6] *Cooperation—What Is It and Why Do It?*, *supra* at 17–18.

> as much as they enjoy conflict. Some lawyers may also be operating under the impression that their clients are impressed by shows of aggression. In addition, combative pretrial behavior may be an attempt to avoid or postpone something that some lawyers fear, and that is an actual trial on the merits.[7]

Judge Waxse's advice on how to be cooperative reminds me of the advice given by Robert Fulghum in his bestseller *All I Really Need to Know I Learned in Kindergarten*:

> All I really need to know about how to live and what to do and how to be, I learned in kindergarten. Wisdom was not at the top of the graduate-school mountain, but there in the sand pile at Sunday School. These are the things I learned. These are the things you already know:
>
> Share everything.
> Play fair.
> Don't hit people.
> Put things back where you found them.
> Clean up your own mess.
> Don't take things that aren't yours.
> Say you're sorry when you hurt somebody.

"Play fair" is something you often say to the spoiled child. That directive seems especially appropriate to the practice of law. As I have pointed out in the last chapter, Rule 3.4 of the ABA Model Rules of Professional Conduct entitled *Fairness to Opposing Party and Counsel*, is designed to require simple fairness. That includes the ethical duty not to "make a frivolous discovery request or fail to make reasonably diligent effort to comply with a legally proper discovery request by an opposing party." Cooperation in law is not just an academic exercise—it is an ethical imperative. We must implement this directive in an adult fashion and overcome the childish inclinations and aggressive tendencies that most of us litigators have.

---

[7] *Id.* at 12.

UNCOOPERATIVE LAWYERS ARE *PER SE* UNETHICAL

Judge Waxse recognizes that cooperation in discovery is not an ideal; rather, it is a baseline ethical imperative. In private correspondence with him on this topic, he told me that:

> Cooperation has to be considered as part of a lawyer's professionalism responsibility. Too many lawyers today are too focused on making money and forgetting their professional responsibilities. As the preamble to the Model Rules says:
>
> > [1] A lawyer, as a member of the legal profession, is a representative of clients, an officer of the legal system and a public citizen having special responsibility for the quality of justice.
>
> That includes the following:
>
> > [6] As a public citizen, a lawyer should seek improvement of the law, access to the legal system, the administration of justice and the quality of service rendered by the legal profession.
>
> Cooperation in litigation is a way to improve "the administration of justice and the quality of the service rendered by the legal profession" and a way obtain the "just, speedy and inexpensive determination" of the dispute.

These sentiments are spelled out in Judge Waxse's article with specific references to our rules of ethics. He begins with an important history lesson. In 1983, the ABA adopted the Model Rules of Professional Conduct. In doing so, it removed the duty of *zealous advocacy* that had appeared in Canon 7 of the predecessor Model Code of Professional Responsibility from Rule 1.3. Apparently, many firms did not get that memo. The ethics rule was modified after much debate and for good reason. Canon 7 of the predecessor Model Code of Professional Responsibility was entitled *A Lawyer Should Represent a Client Zealously Within the Bounds of the Law.* Rule 1.3, adopted in 1983 said, and still says: "A lawyer shall act with reasonable diligence and promptness in representing a client."

As Judge Waxse points out, even before the 1983 change, Canon 7, Ethical Consideration [EC 7-39], discussed cooperation and put zealous advocacy in perspective. It stated:

> In the final analysis, proper functioning of the adversary system depends upon cooperation between lawyers and tribunals in utilizing procedures which will preserve the impartiality of tribunals and make their decisional processes prompt and just, without impinging upon the obligation of lawyers to represent their clients zealously within the framework of the law.[8]

Even with the tempering comments, lawyers focused too much on the zealous advocacy parts. They used it as an excuse to cover "spoiled brat" behavior that made a mockery of cooperation. For this reason, the zealous duties language was eliminated in 1983 and replaced by the more mature and responsible dictates of *diligence* and *promptness.* As Judge Waxse points out, after that adoption, *zealous advocacy* was only mentioned in the preamble:

> [1] A lawyer, as a member of the legal profession, is a representative of clients, an officer of the legal system and a public citizen having special responsibility for the quality of justice.
>
> [2] As a representative of clients, a lawyer performs various functions. As advisor, a lawyer provides a client with an informed understanding of the client's legal rights and obligations and explains their practical implications. As advocate, a lawyer zealously asserts the client's position under the rules of the adversary system. As negotiator, a lawyer seeks a result advantageous to the client but consistent with requirements of honest dealings with others. As an evaluator, a lawyer acts by examining a client's legal affairs and reporting about them to the client or to others.[9]

---

[8] *Model Code of Professional Responsibility*, EC 7-39 (1980).
[9] *Model Rules of Professional Conduct,* Preamble.

Together with the adoption of Rule 1.3, the adopted comment to that rule mentioned *zealous advocacy* and explained its limits:

> A lawyer must also act with commitment and dedication to the interests of the client and with zeal in advocacy upon the client's behalf. A lawyer is not bound, however, to press for every advantage that might be realized for a client.[10]

Again, many lawyers just do not understand. They act like bullies and try to justify their behavior as zealous advocacy. They need to better understand the lessons of kindergarten, as Robert Fulghum said in *All I Really Need to Know I Learned in Kindergarten*:

> What we learn in kindergarten comes up again and again in our lives as long as we live. In far more complex, polysyllabic forms, to be sure. In lectures, encyclopedias, bibles, company rules, courts of law, sermons, and handbooks. Life will examine us continually to see if we have understood and have practiced what we were taught that first year of school.

Judge Waxse analyzed why cooperation and "playing fair" seem so difficult to many litigators. He concluded that it is both the overaggressive personality disorder common to litigators, combined with a basic misunderstanding of ethics:

> There are numerous reasons why cooperation is often not happening. One is the misconception I have already discussed—that lawyers have an ethical obligation of zealous advocacy in every aspect of litigation. Another reason is that lawyers who become litigators often have personalities that love conflict and competition.[11]

Judge Waxse goes on to mention a third reason, greed, that I also examine in my law review article, *Lawyers Behaving Badly*.[12] Judge Waxse observes:

---

[10] *Model Rules of Professional Conduct* 1.3, cmt [1].
[11] *Cooperation—What Is It and Why Do It?*, *supra* at 12.
[12] 60 Mercer L. Rev. 983 (Spring 2009).

> Another reason that is not openly discussed often is that the hourly billing system used by many law firms is an incentive to engage in conflict instead of cooperation. It takes more time to fight over everything than it takes to cooperate. Thus, when the lawyer is paid based solely on how much time they spend working, there is a disincentive to cooperate and therefore a potential conflict with the client's interest in resolving the litigation in a cost effective manner.[13]

Judge Waxse does not mention another greed factor—the big money involved for lawyers in contingency cases. The prospect of making millions of dollars can often tempt otherwise reasonable people into bad behavior. The greed factor is often exasperated by the tendency to automatically vilify the other side—or its close cousin, to vilify all plaintiffs' lawyers or all defense lawyers. It is an unfair bias. Lawyers sitting on both sides of the courtroom can easily fall into this trap. Do not stereotype opposing counsel. See them as people, as individuals, and treat them with respect, not abuse. As Robert Fulghum said:

> Yelling at living things does tend to kill the spirit in them. Sticks and stones may break our bones, but words will break our hearts.

JUDGE WAXSE'S RULE-BASED SOLUTION

After pointing out that cooperation is an ethical imperative, Judge Waxse's new article provides practical, rule-based advice on how to make cooperation happen—even when faced with spoiled, scorpion-type noncooperators. His advice is directed to both lawyers and judges. Indeed, cooperation is impossible in dealing with hopeless bickerers unless judges provide adult guidance and a stern hand. Judge Waxse begins by pointing to Rule 16(a), where a judge can and should be "establishing early and continuing control so that the case will not be protracted because of lack of management" and "discouraging wasteful pretrial activities."

---

[13] *Cooperation—What Is It and Why Do It?*, *supra* at 12.

Next, Judge Waxse pointed to Rule 26(b)(2)(C) (pre-2015 amendments), where a judge is required to limit discovery in certain instances where the parties cannot cooperate enough to do it on their own. In that situation where counsel for one side, or for both sides, cannot cooperate, Judge Waxse reminds judges that Rule 26(b)(2)(C) allows them on motion or their own initiative to "limit the frequency or extent of discovery otherwise allowed." There are a variety of grounds to so limit discovery under Rule 26(b)(2)(B), including disproportionate burden compared to benefit, the so-called *proportionality principle*. This argument is also now available under Rule 26(b)(1).

Judge Waxse then refers to the duties lawyers have under Rule 26(f) to work together in good faith to agree on a plan of discovery for the case and to discuss "the nature and basis of their claims and defenses." Next, Rule 26(g) "allows the court to insure that lawyers are not being uncooperative by making improper discovery requests and responses."[14] Judge Waxse points out, as Judge Grimm did before him in *Mancia,* that Rule 26(g)(3) provides courts with a strong enforcement tool to punish uncooperative lawyers for making an improper discovery request, response, or objection. Judge Waxse notes that a judge could go even further and punish lawyers who act like petulant children by using 28 U.S.C. Section 1927, which states:

> Any attorney or other person admitted to conduct cases in any court of the United States or any Territory thereof who so multiplies the proceedings in any case unreasonably and vexatiously may be required by the court to satisfy personally the excess costs, expenses, and attorneys' fees reasonably incurred because of such conduct.

Judge Waxse sums up by saying that the rules and the enforcement statute "provide a clear path to cooperation." In other words, Judge Waxse is saying what every parent knows—that clear, consistent, and firm discipline is the only solution to a petulant child. A judge must be ready to step in and provide adult supervision, including punishment of an uncooperative lawyer. In some cases, a judge may even have to impose monetary sanctions against an attorney personally. A judge

---

[14] *Cooperation—What Is It and Why Do It?, supra* at 14.

may have to use Section 1927 to force him or her to pay the fees and costs that the other side incurs because of their vexatious conduct.

CONCLUSION

Although I did not follow the maxim of "spare the rod, spoil the child" when raising my children (I personally think that is barbaric), I never hesitated to take away their allowance (or computers and other toys) and impose other monetary sanctions. Judges should be prepared to provide the same kind of tough love in their courtrooms to lawyers who do not cooperate.

Cooperation must always be a two-way street. It must never mean capitulation to a bully. We all know that some lawyers are like spoiled children and are incapable of cooperation. They are incapable of reasonable dialogue. It is either their way or the highway—take it or leave it. When you are unfortunate enough to have attorneys like that as your opposing counsel, cooperation is impossible without strong judicial involvement. It is as simple as that.

When one attorney refuses to cooperate, the judge *must* step in and enforce the rules and the statute in order to make the other side cooperate. Judge Waxse points out how the rules and Section 1927 "provide a clear path to cooperation." However, that path only works if there is a wise judge with the intestinal fortitude necessary to enforce those rules and statute against sometimes very powerful uncooperative attorneys.

If a judge will not step in, who will? The bully must not be allowed to make a mockery of justice. Our whole system of justice depends on enforcement of the law—even, or perhaps especially, when the enforcement is against lawyers. Judges, make your courtroom a bully-free zone!

For judges to fulfill their duty, they must, of course, first take care to find out what is really going on in a case. They should not simply assume that both sides are to blame. That just rewards the petulant, the bullies who try to blame the other side ("he started it!"). Judges need to take the time to determine which counsel is a *bona fide* cooperator and which is a poser. It may sometimes be the case that both sides are phonies and neither are cooperative. It may also be the case that only one side is uncooperative. It may take a series of hearings to sort things out. However, when a judge recognizes a one-sided, playground-bully situation, the judge must act decisively. Fulfillment of the purpose of Rule 1 *FRCP*—to attain the just, speedy, and inexpensive determination of every action—depends on this judicial action.

As a final thought, I leave you with the words of Robert Fulghum, who, strangely enough, kind of looks like Judge Waxse with a bowtie. As a person over 60, I can certainly resonate with these observations. No matter what your age, perhaps you can too.

> My convictions have validity for me because I have experimented with the compounds of ideas of others in the laboratory of my mind. And I've tested the results in the living out of my life. At twenty-one, I had drawn an abstract map based on the evidence of others. At sixty, I have accumulated a practical guide grounded in my own experience. At twenty-one, I could discuss transportation theory with authority. At sixty, I know which bus to catch to go where, what the fare is, and how to get back home again. It is not my bus, but I know how to use it.[15]

[15]Robert Fulghum, *Words I Wish I Wrote* (1997)—Note–Published April 7, 1999 by Harper Perennial (first published 1997).

17 e-Discovery Gamers: Join Me in Stopping Them

Many lawyers view litigation as just a game, but a game to be won at all costs. Electronic discovery is just part of the game. The goal for such lawyers is not justice and certainly not truth. The goal is to win the game by any means possible. The game is about the personal profit and power that comes from winning, either by final judgment or settlement. Law gamers do not care about justice. They are only in it for the money.

TRUTH IS NOT JUST A CONSTRUCT

Gamer lawyers do not see e-discovery as a way to get at the truth of a dispute. They do not care about the truth. Nongamers ask for and look at documents to try to find out what really happened, but not gamers. They view facts as malleable. E-discovery for them is just a way to find enough documents to construct a story. They only care about whether a story will likely persuade a judge or jury to rule in their client's favor, not whether it is true.

Gamers view requests for discovery as potentially dangerous to their constructs. For that reason, they will play endless, elaborate games to try to hide the facts. For them, hide-the-ball is just a game—one that might have economic consequences if they are caught, but they rarely are. So, the games go on.

E-DISCOVERY CREATES LEVERAGE

Gamer lawyers use discovery, especially e-discovery, as a way to impose an economic burden on the other side—the person or persons who they are playing against. If they can make document production expensive enough, they can increase their leverage. They can drive up the settlement value of a case. They can win and so make more money.

Conversely, if they dump a big enough pile of nearly irrelevant documents on the requesting party, they can place a counter-burden. This burden of review creates an economic impact. It may also be a good way to hide-the-ball—a smart move for a true gamer. Gamer lawyers play on both sides, plaintiff and defense. Greed is an equal opportunity employer.

GAMERS AND GAMESMANSHIP

Gamer lawyers tend to think that all lawyers are gamers like them, but they just do not play as well. They assume that you have as little regard for the truth as they do. They assume that you, like them, are just trying to win at all costs. They assume you are trying to hide the ball just as much as they are. They assume your requests for production are as exaggerated and extortions-oriented as theirs.

If someone, especially an opposing counsel, calls them on their gamesmanship, they think that also is just another game tactic. They tend to view all lawyers who call them on their gamesmanship as just irritated gamers or spoiled sports. No doubt that is what they are thinking about me right now.

When gamers do sometimes realize that the other side is hamstrung by rules and is not a gamer like they are, they tend to think that they are up against a naive patsy and play even harder. Nothing gets them off their game. They are delighted when their adversary is a moralist. They are more than happy to take advantage of that. A true gamer does not care about rules of any kind. Rules are meant to be broken, if you can get away with it. Cheating is just another game tactic. Gamers only care about winning. They find it hard to believe that everyone is not in it just for the money.

DO YOU THINK GAMERS ARE A MINORITY?

Fortunately, in my experience, litigators with that kind of win-at-all-costs mind view are a small minority. Nevertheless, they are often very successful. What do you think? How common do you think this amoral attitude is among litigators?

ARE GAMERS UNPROFESSIONAL MONEY GRUBBERS?

I personally consider the mindview or *gestalt* of gamer lawyers to be an overcompetitive plebeian view of litigation. I consider them to be unprofessional and unethical because this approach exalts winning and personal profit over the duty of a lawyer to serve as an officer of the court. To me, this service of justice is a near-sacred duty. This is why I became a lawyer—not to make money or amass power, and certainly not just to play games. What do you think? Am I just a naive idealist? An irritated gamer?

GAMES, GAMERS, AND GAME THEORY

After all of this, it may surprise you to know that I myself am a gamer. I like games, especially video games, and I even find game theory somewhat interesting. I have been playing games all of my life and computer games since *Pong*. The first computer programs that I ever wrote in the early 1980s were games, mostly for my kids. They still remember my *Mr. Computer Head*, the world's first make-a-face program, which I created on my Texas Instrument 99/4A using TI basic, assembly language, and some machine code. It had color graphics, music, some animation, and moving pixels (sprites). It even had one of the first speech synthesizers. After you assembled a face, Mr. Computer Head would smile approvingly and say, "I sure look good now." It was fun creating and playing. I don't have time to play much these days, but I still keep up with the latest thing.

Yes, I love games, but only when there are rules. Without them, it is just anarchy. Moreover, as an adult, I know that there is a time and a place for games and gamesmanship. Litigation is not the time or the place. Truth and justice are more important than winning. Making a contribution to society is more important than making money.

I am also interested in game theory, although I am no expert on it. Game theory is the study of strategic decision-making. It focuses on the interplay of conflict and cooperation; for this reason, it is a natural topic for legal analysis.

GROSSMAN AND CORMACK ON GAME THEORY, ETHICS, AND E-DISCOVERY

The role of game theory in e-discovery was considered in an article by Maura Grossman and Gordon Cormack.[1] This article has been a sleeper, but it is well worth reading for the game theory discussion alone (although this is just one part of their interesting article on ethics and search).

The ethical issues involved in *Some Thoughts* are evidence search-specific. It considers the ethics of a responding party who might wish to "game the system" by deliberate use of ineffective search and review methods. It also considers the ethics of a requesting party who might wish to, in their words:

> game the system *by deliberate use of* overly broad requests for production, either to hide the true nature of the information being sought, or to ensure that the pertinent data are produced, even if the responding party is less than diligent in its search efforts.[2]

The bottom line for me on game theory and e-discovery is that it shows that any purely rational approach to discovery—one that disregards ethics and good faith—is doomed to failure. It is a game that cannot be won. I base this conclusion on what is called the *prisoner's dilemma* in game theory. Here is how Grossman and Cormack explained it:

> The "litigator's dilemma" referenced in the second quotation above refers to the well-known characterization of discovery as an example of the hypothetical scenario from game theory, the

---

[1]Maura Grossman and Gordon Cormack, *Some Thoughts on Incentives, Rules, and Ethics Concerning the Use of Search Technology in E-Discovery,* 12 SEDONA CONF. J. 89–104 (2011) (hereinafter "*Some Thoughts*").
[2]*Some Thoughts* at 95.

> "prisoner's dilemma," in which there is mutual advantage to both parties in pursuing common interests so long as both act cooperatively and in good faith, but tremendous disadvantage to the party that acts cooperatively and in good faith, if the other does not. There is a lesser disadvantage—but a disadvantage nonetheless—if both parties act uncooperatively and in bad faith. According to game theory, the "rational choice" in this situation is for each party to act uncooperatively and in bad faith, incurring the lesser disadvantage, so as to avoid the risk of the more severe disadvantage. Although the end result is disadvantageous to both (relative to acting cooperatively and in good faith), the disadvantage is less than would be incurred by one party behaving well, when the other party behaves poorly. Uncertainty, fear, and distrust tend to preclude the mutually advantageous outcome....
>
> Whether or not e-discovery truly is a prisoner's dilemma, the belief that it is may be self-fulfilling—with the effect of incentivizing counsel for either party to engage in bad behavior, in the belief that it is the rational choice under the circumstances.[3]

Grossman and Cormack end their article with the following conclusion:

> Whether in the capacity of counsel for the responding party, counsel for the requesting party, or as an officer of the court, a lawyer has many incentives to conduct an efficient and effective search. Incentives to conduct an ineffective or inefficient search arise largely from attempts to game the system, fear that an adversary will game the system, insufficient knowledge of the efficacy and cost of available search methods, and financial profit from the use (or failure to use) particular search methods. By and large, these incentives tend to be neutralized by the existing rules and ethical proscriptions when counsel are knowledgeable and competent with respect to search methods in e-discovery and strategies for their optimal use. The net

[3] *Some Thoughts* at 96–97.

effect is that the approach most beneficial to the client, and to the justice system, as well as least likely to violate the rules or ethical proscriptions, is to make an informed choice of the most effective, most efficient search method. Lawyers should not assume or insist that existing practices—such as exhaustive manual review—are always the best choice in the face of growing evidence that other methods can achieve as good, if not better results, at a fraction of the cost.[4]

CONCLUSION

Litigation is not a game. It is an important governmental process central to our democratic system. Law is not a mere business. It is an important profession, a calling. Truth and justice—law and ethics—are core cultural values.

Lawyers who ignore these values and employ game tactics are doomed to fail. If their opposition is also a gamer, then both will lie and cheat each other. The clients on both sides will lose. If their opposition is not a gamer, they will also lose as soon as the judge who controls the proceeding catches on to their gamesmanship. Once they are exposed, they are done. You can easily stop unethical gamers by exposing them.

My message to lawyer gamers is this: Quit the game. Play video games instead. If you just went into law to make money, get out. Go into business. They have different ethics and different rules. You can win there—maybe—but you cannot win here. The profession, especially the judges, will make sure of that, as will thousands of lawyers like me. We care about the law, even if you don't.

[4] *Id.* at 103.

18

Attorneys Admonished by Judge Nolan Not to "Confuse Advocacy with Adversarial Conduct" and Instructed on the Proportionality Doctrine

I suggest that all lawyers and others involved with e-discovery become familiar with an order by U.S. Magistrate Judge Nan R. Nolan that begins by admonishing counsel "not to confuse advocacy with adversarial conduct."[1] This opinion from a jurist who is well known for kindness and e-discovery expertise advances the jurisprudence on the all-important best practice of *cooperation*. This is the fifth step of the attorney-centric electronic discovery best practices (EDBP) workflow chart.[2]

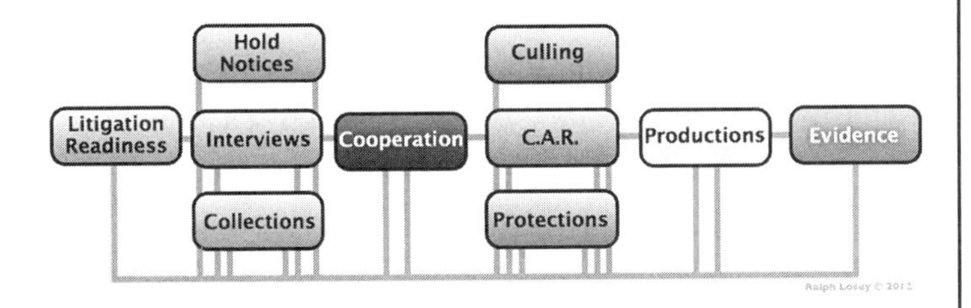

The *Kleen Products* opinion also provides an excellent collection of legal authority on a basic component for cooperation, namely proportionality. This was kind of a

[1]Kleen Products, LLC v. Packaging Corp. of America, 10 C 5711 (N.D. Ill. Sept. 28, 2012).
[2]*See http://www.EDBP.com.*

legacy order for Judge Nolan because she retired on October 1, 2012, just days after this opinion was issued.

Judge Nolan concluded this opinion with three specific best practice suggestions, which have already been incorporated into the cooperation page of the EDBP website. Furthermore, all of the best practices developed by the Seventh Circuit Electronic Discovery Committee, with which Judge Nolan is actively involved, were set forth in their *Principles Relating to the Discovery of Electronically Stored Information* (Rev. Aug. 1, 2010) and have also been included on the EDBP website, as have the New York State Bar Association's *Best Practices in E-Discovery in New York State and Federal Courts* (2011).

COOPERATION IN DISCOVERY IS AN ETHICAL IMPERATIVE

Judge Nolan begins her opinion with a quote from the Sedona Conference *Cooperation Proclamation:*

> Lawyers have twin duties of loyalty: While they are retained to be zealous advocates for their clients, they bear a professional obligation to conduct discovery in a diligent and candid manner. Their combined duty is to strive in the best interests of their clients to achieve the best results at a reasonable cost, with integrity and candor as officers of the court. Cooperation does not conflict with the advancement of their clients' interests—it enhances it. Only when lawyers confuse advocacy with adversarial conduct are these twin duties in conflict.[3]

So many lawyers do not understand this, especially the ones my age (sixties) who were raised in a culture of litigation as war. They seem to have forgotten the oaths they swore long ago when first admitted to the bar and allowed to practice as officers of the court. They seem to have forgotten their basic ethical duties of candor to the tribunal[4]—not to mention their ethical duty under Rule 3.2 to expedite

[3] 10 Sedona Conf. J. 331, 331 (2009).

[4] *See* ABA Model Rule of Professional Responsibility, Rule 3.3, Candor Toward Tribunal.

litigation and duty under Rule 4-3.4 of fairness to opposing party and counsel.

COOPERATION IN DISCOVERY IS REQUIRED BY RULES OF PROCEDURE

Many attorneys and judges also seem to have forgotten what Judge Paul Grimm in *Mancia* called the most misunderstood and underutilized Federal Rule of Civil Procedure, Rule 26(g).[5] Rule 26(g) is the Rule 11 of discovery. Under Rule 26(g), an attorney's signature on a discovery request or response "certifies" that the request is reasonable, the disclosure is complete and correct, and the discovery is "not interposed for any improper purpose, such as to harass, cause unnecessary delay, or needlessly increase the cost of litigation."

As Judge Grimm's *Mancia* opinion goes on to explain in great detail, cooperation in discovery is not only required by professional ethics but also by many of our rules of civil procedure, including especially Rule 1.[6]

PLAINTIFFS' MOTIONS IN *KLEEN PRODUCTS*

After beginning the opinion with the quote from *Cooperation Proclamation,* Judge Nolan goes on to explain the series of discovery motions filed at that time in this very large class action antitrust case:

- Plaintiffs' Motion to Compel Defendants to Produce Documents and Data from All Reasonable Accessible Sources
- Plaintiffs' Motion to Compel Temple-Inland to Include Additional Document Custodians

---

[5]Mancia v. Mayflower Textile Services Co., 253 F.R.D. 354 (D. Md. 2008).

[6]*Also see* Gensler, *The Bull's-Eye View of Cooperation in Discovery*, 10 SEDONA CONF. J. 363, at 363 (2009 Supp.); Sedona Conference, *The Case for Cooperation*, 10 SEDONA CONF. J. 339 (2009 Supp.); Ralph Losey, *Mancia v. Mayflower Begins a Pilgrimage to the New World of Cooperation,* 10 SEDONA CONF. J. 377 (2009 Supp.); J. Waxse, *Cooperation—What Is It and Why Do It?*, XVIII RICH. J. L. & TECH. 8 (2012).

- Plaintiffs' Motion to Compel International Paper Company to Include Additional Document Custodians
- Defendant Georgia-Pacific LLC's Motion for Protective Order

Judge Nolan then goes on to recount the other discovery issues that the parties had previously resolved without her having to enter an order. However, Judge Nolan did have many, many, hearings on these issues and made highly suggestive statements of her thoughts—statements that indicated how she would probably rule.

The biggest dispute the parties resolved after days and days of help by Judge Nolan concerned predictive coding. This is the much discussed dispute where the plaintiffs were trying to force the defendants into a "redo" of their prior search and production that did not use predictive coding. The plaintiffs claimed that the keyword search used by defendants likely only found 25 percent of the relevant documents, whereas a predictive coding search would likely retrieve 70 percent.

The plaintiffs had a good argument from an abstract point of view, but it was flawed procedurally. It came too late, after the plaintiffs' production was substantially complete. Plus, as Judge Nolan pointedly observed in the hearings to help persuade the plaintiffs to back off:

> Sedona Principle 6, "[r]esponding parties are best situated to evaluate the procedures, methodologies, and techniques appropriate for preserving and producing their own electronically stored information." *See* the Sedona Conference, *The Sedona Conference Best Practices Commentary on the Use of Search and Information Retrieval Methods in E-Discovery*, 8 SEDONA CONF. J. 189, 193 (Fall 2007).

The plaintiffs wanted to use the latest new-age methods of search, but they approached the problem with decidedly old-school adversarial methods. It was an odd mix doomed to failure. You have got to have both, especially when you are in front of a sophisticated, Sedona-schooled judge like Nan Nolan. If you are really after truth and justice in today's world of exponentially growing ESI and not just playing a refashioned game of "hassle the other side," both your technology and your culture need to be "new age." As Jason R. Baron put it:

> [T]he challenge is how best to reasonably (not perfectly) manage the exponentially growing amount of ESI caught in, and subject to, modern-day discovery practice. The answer lies principally in culture change (i.e., fostering cooperation strategies), combined with savvier exploitation of a range of sophisticated software and analytical techniques.[7]

INTERROGATORY SIX AND PROPORTIONALITY

Even though the predictive coding battle settled, many other discovery disputes remained, including the defendant Georgia-Pacific LLC's Motion for Protective Order. In this motion, Judge Nolan was asked to quash the plaintiffs' Sixth Interrogatory. The interrogatory requested various background information over an eight-year period for each of the approximately 400 persons on the litigation-hold list. The defendant claimed that this request was too burdensome, would take 800 hours to try to answer, and specified the details of what would be required. The plaintiffs responded by saying that the Sixth Interrogatory "is hardly burdensome" and can be "answered by a small production of paper."[8]

The court did not buy the plaintiffs' argument. In fact, Judge Nolan found it disingenuous and invoked the all-important proportionality constraints that govern all discovery. Here is her ruling:

> First, issuing the Sixth Interrogatory within days of receiving the list of litigation-hold recipients violated the spirit of cooperation that this Court has encouraged the parties to pursue....
>
> Second, GP has established an undue burden in responding to the Sixth Interrogatory. "All discovery is subject to the limitations imposed by Rule 26(b)(2)(C)." Fed. R. Civ. P. 26(b)(1). The Rule 26 proportionality test allows the Court to "limit

---

[7] Jason R. Baron, *Law in the Age of Exabytes*, XVII Rich. J.L. & Tech. 5 (2011).
[8] *Id.* at 17.

> discovery if it determines that the burden of the discovery outweighs its benefit." *In re IKB Deutsche Industriebank AG,*No. 09 CV 7582, 2010 WL 1526070, at *5 (N.D. Ill. Apr. 8, 2010). Rule 26(b)(2)(C)(iii) requires a court to limit discovery if it determines that "the burden or expense of the proposed discovery outweighs its likely benefit, considering the needs of the case, the amount in controversy, the parties' resources, the importance of the issues at stake in the action, and the importance of the discovery in resolving the issues." In other words, "Rule 26(b)(2)(C)(iii) empowers a court to limit the frequency or extent of discovery if it determines that the burden or expense of the proposed discovery outweighs its likely benefit or that it is unreasonably cumulative or duplicative." *Sommerfield v. City of Chicago*, 613 F. Supp. 2d 1004, 1017 (N.D. Ill. 2009) objections overruled, 06 C 3132, 2010 WL 780390 (N.D. Ill. Mar. 3, 2010). "The 'metrics' set forth in Rule 26(b)(2)(C)(iii) provide courts significant flexibility and discretion to assess the circumstances of the case and limit discovery accordingly to ensure that the scope and duration of discovery is reasonably proportional to the value of the requested information, the needs of the case, and the parties' resources." The Sedona Conference, *The Sedona Conference Commentary on Proportionality in Electronic Discovery*, 11 SEDONA CONF. J. 289, 294 (2010); *see Sommerfield*, 613 F. Supp. 2d at 1017 ("The application of Rule 26(b)(2)(C)(iii) involves a highly discretionary determination based upon an assessment of a number of competing considerations.").[9]

As a strong proponent of proportionality I was glad to see Judge Nolan add to the growing jurisprudence in this area.

CUSTODIAN COUNT AND PROPORTIONALITY

There was also a battle over scope of discovery centered around custodians. The plaintiffs wanted the ESI of 35 more custodians from two defendants. The defendants were willing to add 30 more custodians,

[9] *Id.* at 19, 20.

but they wanted limits on the sources of ESI that would be included for the additional custodians.

Judge Nolan begins her analysis of this issue by noting that antitrust cases take an "expansive view of relevance" and allow for "broad discovery."[10] However, she also noted once again the importance of proportionality (note this is before the 2015 amendments):

> However, "[a]ll discovery, even if otherwise permitted by the Federal Rules of Civil Procedure because it is likely to yield relevant evidence, is subject to the court's obligation to balance its utility against its cost." *U.S. ex rel. McBride v. Halliburton Co.*, 272 F.R.D. 235, 240 (D.D.C. 2011) (Facciola, M.J.); *see* Fed. R. Civ. P. 26(b)(2)(C).[11]

The plaintiffs argued that the proposed additional custodians and ESI sources should be included because they were all senior executives with responsibilities over the pricing issues in the case who "exchanged an unusually large" number of e-mails with top sales and marketing executives already named as custodians.[12] Judge Nolan rejected this argument:

> But just because a proposed custodian exchanged a large number of emails with a current custodian does not mean that the proposed custodians will have a significant number of important, non-cumulative information. Further, until Plaintiffs have had an opportunity to review the huge quantity of information already produced from the existing custodians, it is difficult for the Court to determine the utility of the proposed discovery. *See McBride*, 272 F.R.D. at 241 ("Without any showing of the significance of the non-produced e-mails, let alone the likelihood of finding the 'smoking gun,' the [party's] demands [for additional custodians] cannot possibly be justified when one balances its cost against its utility."); *Jones v. Nat'l Council of Young Men's Christian Ass'ns of the United States*,

---

[10] *Id.* at 27.
[11] *Id.* at 28.
[12] *Id.* at 29.

> No. 09 C 6437, 2011 WL 7568591, at *2 (N.D. Ill. Oct. 21, 2011) ("The Court finds that Plaintiffs' untargeted, all-encompassing request fails to focus on key individuals and the likelihood of receiving relevant information."); *Garcia v. Tyson Foods, Inc.*, No. 06-2198, 2010 WL 5392660, at *14 (D. Kan. Dec. 21, 2010) (Waxse, M.J.) ("Plaintiffs present no evidence that a search of e-mail repositories of the 11 employees at issue is likely to reveal any additional responsive e-mails.... Plaintiffs must present something more than mere speculation that responsive e-mails might exist in order for this Court to compel the searches and productions requested.").[13]

Judge Nolan also pointed out that one of the two defendants at issue here had already produced the ESI of 75 custodians, and the other of 28 custodians. However, she also noted:

> [T]he selection of custodians is more than a mathematical count. The selection of custodians must be designed to respond fully to document requests and to produce responsive, nonduplicative documents during the relevant period. *See, generally, Eisai Inc. v. Sanofi-Aventis U.S., LLC*, No. 08-4168, 2012 WL 1299379, at *9 (D.N.J. April 16, 2012).[14]

Judge Nolan then goes on to grant the plaintiffs' motion to compel, in part because the two defendants failed to back up their allegations of undue burden with specific facts:

> While a discovery request can be denied if the "burden or expense of the proposed discovery outweighs its likely benefit," Fed. R. Civ. P. 26(b)(2)(C)(iii), a party objecting to discovery must specifically demonstrate how the request is burdensome. *See Heraeus Kulzer, GmbH v. Biomet, Inc.*, 633 F.3d 591, 598 (7th Cir. 2011); *Sauer v. Exelon Generation Co.*, No. 10 C 3258, 2011 WL 3584780, at *5 (N.D. Ill. Aug. 15, 2011). This specific showing can include "an estimate of the number of documents that it would be required to provide ... the number of hours of

[13] *Id.* at 30.
[14] *Id.* at 30–31.

work by lawyers and paralegals required, [or] the expense." *Heraeus Kulzer*, 633 F.3d at 598. Here, TIN's and IP's conclusory statements do not provide evidence in support of their burdensome arguments.[15]

RULE 26(b)(2)(B) AND TIMING

The plaintiffs also sought to compel all defendants to search their backup tapes. The defendants invoked the protection of Rule 26(b)(2)(B), claiming that their backup tapes were not reasonably accessible and that the plaintiffs had not shown good cause to require their production.[16] (Note that after the 2015 amendments, this objection can also be made under Rule 26(b)(1), where accessibility is now a criterion to consider in determining scope of relevance.)

Judge Nolan begins her analysis of this straightforward dispute by analysis of existing case law on 26(b)(2)(B). She also examines case law dealing with backup tapes. It is a good collection of legal authorities on both the general and specific issues.

The defendants here did more than make general allegations of burden. They submitted affidavits showing costs just to restore their tapes, ranging from a high of $1 million for one defendant to a low of *only* $200,000 for another. The plaintiffs disputed these cost estimates and suggested that the defendants could reduce the tape restoration costs by "sampling the media to determine whether they contain responsive nonduplicative information."[17]

Judge Nolan sidestepped these issues by holding that the plaintiffs' motion was premature. She noted that "there is no discovery cutoff date in this case, and plaintiffs are only 20 percent complete with their first level review of Defendants' documents."[18] Judge Nolan ordered the plaintiffs to complete their review of the readily accessible ESI produced

---

[15] *Id.* at 32.
[16] *Id.* at 35.
[17] *Id.* at 37.
[18] *Id.*

before clamoring for production of inaccessible data. This is in accord with the rules and commentary thereon:

> The volume of—and the ability to search—much electronically stored information means that in many cases the responding party will be able to produce information from reasonably accessible sources that will fully satisfy the parties' discovery needs.[19]

Accordingly, Judge Nolan denied plaintiffs' motion to compel without prejudice.

CONCLUSION

Judge Nan Nolan, who is a great lover of art and always embodies the "glass half-full" attitude, concluded the *Kleen Products* order on a positive note. She points to a number of courts that have already "instituted model orders to assist counsel in transitioning to the cooperative discovery approach."[20]

Judge Nolan then draws three lessons from *Kleen Products* about cooperation:

> First, the approach should be started early in the case. It is difficult or impossible to unwind procedures that have already been implemented. Second, in multiple party cases represented by separate counsel, it may be beneficial for liaisons to be assigned to each party. Finally, to the extent possible, discovery phases should be discussed and agreed to at the onset of discovery.[21]

Judge Nolan concludes by calling upon all attorneys to conduct discovery in a cooperative manner, which she calls a *paradigm shift.*

> The Cooperation Proclamation calls for a "paradigm shift" in how parties engage in the discovery process. The Sedona

[19] Fed. R. Civ. P. 26(b)(2), Advisory Committee's note (2006).
[20] Seventh Circuit Electronic Discovery Pilot Program, *Model Standing Order*; Southern District of New York Pilot Program; District of Delaware, *Default Standard for Discovery.*
[21] *Id.* at 39.

> Conference, *The Sedona Conference Cooperation Proclamation*, 10 Sedona Conf. J. 331, 332–33 (2009). In some small way, it is hoped that this Opinion can be of some help to others interested in pursuing a cooperative approach. The Court commends the lawyers and their clients for conducting their discovery obligations in a collaborative manner.

Unfortunately, Judge Nan Nolan is correct in endorsing the Sedona paradigm-shift observation. I say *unfortunately* because, unlike Judge Nolan, I sometimes see the glass half-empty. Because long-standing rules of ethics and civil procedure have always required cooperative discovery, what does the paradigm-shift observation say about our existing legal system?

The Increasing Importance of Rule 26(g) to Control e-Discovery Abuses

19

A federal judge in Baltimore added teeth to Rule 26(g) with an opinion that enforced the mandatory sanctions provision of the rule.[1] This appears to have been the first published ruling of its kind. That is amazing when you consider that subsection (g) of Rule 26 went into effect in 1983. This well-intentioned rule has been hidden in the sands of time, toothless, for many years. It might have remained buried and forgotten forever, but for an opinion in 2008 by then Magistrate Judge Paul Grimm.[2] Judge Grimm exposed Rule 26(g) to the e-discovery world and called it the most underutilized and misunderstood rule in the book. However, even Judge Grimm in *Mancia* did not actually use Rule 26(g) to impose sanctions. He used it in *Mancia* as a side note to his main theme of cooperation.[3]

Judge Grimm was right about 26(g) being a stealth rule. It went into effect in 1983. There was a brief flurry of

---

[1]Branhaven LLC v. Beeftek, Inc., 288 F.R.D. 386, (D. Md. 2013).

[2]Mancia v. Mayflower Textile Services Co., 253 F.R.D. 354 (D. Md. 2008).

[3]*Also see* HM Elecs., Inc. v. R.F. Techs., Inc., 2015 WL 4714908, at *1, *12–14, *16, *18, *20 (S.D. Cal. Aug. 7, 2015); Brown v. Tellermate Holdings Ltd., 2014 WL 2987051, at *17–23 (S.D. Ohio July 1, 2014).

interest from some members of the bar and judiciary who were active in rules reform. They hoped the new rule would fulfill its stated purpose of discouraging discovery abuse. Unfortunately, this flurry of interest was not shared by most in the judiciary. After a few initial failures, most practitioners forgot about subsection (g). In my experience, few practitioners ever tried to use 26(g) in litigation before *Mancia*. That is why Rule 26(g) did not have the intended effect to curb discovery abuses.

Before *Mancia,* I had never seen nor heard of a judge enforcing 26(g). I had not focused on subsubsection (3), 26(g)(3), which requires the imposition of sanctions when 26(g) is violated. Trust me, it is violated by sloppy lawyers every day. It is violated every time they sign a form for discovery responses with little or no thought, much less the *reasonable efforts* required by the rules. Here is the mandatory sanctions language of (g)(3):

> (3) Sanction for Improper Certification. If a certification violates this rule without substantial justification, the court, on motion or on its own, must impose an appropriate sanction on the signer, the party on whose behalf the signer was acting, or both. The sanction may include an order to pay the reasonable expenses, including attorney's fees, caused by the violation.

There is no discretion afforded to the judge by the rule. That is highly unusual where sanctions are concerned. There is not even a requirement of bad faith or intent, as there is for any other sanction. Sanctions *must* be imposed upon proof of violation without substantial justification. Yet, has anyone ever heard of a sanction being entered under the rule? I have not, and I've been in litigation since before 1980.

JUDGE GAUVEY ENFORCES THE RULE

Mancia pointed all of this out in 2008. However, unlike technology, the judicial system moves slow. The first published opinion actually enforcing 26(g) did not take place until 5 years after *Mancia* and 30 years after the rule's enactment. It should come as no surprise that the sanctions were imposed by one of Judge Grimm's colleagues on the

Baltimore bench, Magistrate Judge Susan Gauvey.[4] This is a well-reasoned opinion that is filled with good quotes, which you may want to use in your motions. It should be especially handy to cite when going against sloppy opposing counsel. As we all know, there is no shortage of those around, especially when it comes to e-discovery.

The plaintiff's corporation and both of the plaintiff's attorneys—a senior partner and an associate—were sanctioned in *Branhaven.* They were ordered to pay the costs and fees incurred by defense counsel in connection with the plaintiff's "large, disorganized and last minute document production."[5] Judge Gauvey followed the clear language of the rule requiring sanctions:

> The Court has found a violation of the rule without substantial justification and accordingly must impose an appropriate sanction, which in the Court's opinion are the manpower and equipment costs defendants incurred as a result of the last minute and inadequate form and manner of the document production and reasonable attorneys' fees in bringing this violation to the Court's attention.[6]

The financial obligation to pay the costs and fees, with the exact amount to be determined, was made joint and several between the plaintiff and its attorneys. Judge Gauvey has left it to the plaintiff and plaintiff's counsel to sort out between themselves who pays how much. What a situation for a lawyer to be in!

Rule 26(g) is the *Rule 11* of discovery. However, unlike Rule 11, a judge *must* impose sanctions if it is violated. Still, as mentioned, in spite of the rule's terminology, this is the first time I have ever seen a sanction imposed. Thank you, Judge Gauvey, for having the wherewithal to enforce the rule. Unless judges enforce the rules, they do us little good.

---

[4]Branhaven LLC v. Beeftek, Inc., 288 F.R.D. 386 (D. Md. 2013).
[5]*Branhaven* at *1.
[6]*Id.* at *7.

DLA PIPER MAKES THE MOVE

Thanks also goes to DLA Piper, who, as defense counsel, brought the clear violation of the rule by plaintiff's counsel to the attention of the court. Apparently, they were listening to the sage advice of their e-discovery guru, Browning E. Marean. (Browning has since passed away. I was proud to call him a friend and learned much from him over the years.) Although Rule 26(g)(3) allows for *sua sponte* enforcement by the judge, more lawyers need to try to move it along. We need to ask for judges to enforce Rule 26(g). We now have a case on point to help us to do that. Let us follow the pied Piper and join this justice parade. The end result will be a cleaner, more efficient discovery system.

COMPLIANCE WITH RULE 26(g) IS IMPORTANT

Violations of the rule are costly to everyone, as the *Branhaven* opinion clearly shows. However, worse than lost money, violations undercut the core of our system of justice. In the U.S. common law system, the pursuit of truth is in the hands of lawyers, not judges, as it is in the rest of the world using the Napoleonic civil law system. As Judge Gauvey so eloquently put it in her opinion:

> Plaintiff's counsel asserts that "[n]one of Branhaven, Scidera, [or any of plaintiff's counsel] intentionally concealed any discoverable material, nor did we take any actions that were designed to frustrate these proceedings or the discovery process in particular." (ECF No. 59–3, 7, ¶ 27). That, however, is not the standard. As plaintiff's counsel has an affirmative duty to assure that their client responds completely and promptly to discovery requests. Their inaction seriously frustrated the defense of this case. The record here demonstrates a casualness at best and a recklessness at worst in plaintiff's counsel's treatment of their discovery duties. I agree with defense counsel that the attorneys abdicated their responsibilities while representing that they had not. If all counsel operated at this level of disinterest as to discovery obligations, chaos would ensue and the orderliness of the discovery process among counsel in

federal courts, which is exquisitely dependent on honorable attorney self-regulation, would be lost.[7]

THE DUTIES OF COUNSEL OF RECORD UNDER RULE 26 CANNOT BE DELEGATED

Plaintiff's counsel here was a picture of overdelegation. They just asked the client to respond to the defendant's e-discovery requests, and then walked away. "Set it and forget it" is not permitted by the rules. Lawyers must supervise all discovery, especially complicated e-discovery responses. Both the rules and common law make that clear.

In *Branhaven,* the client made a mess of things, forcing the defendant to incur unnecessary expenses and delays. By the way, the answer is not to delegate to an e-discovery vendor either.[8] Only lawyers, counsel of record, can sign discovery responses. They alone are fully responsible, although, of course, a court can sanction the client too, as happened in *Branhaven.*

DUTY OF REASONABLE INQUIRY

Rule 26(g) requires an attorney to certify that he or she has made a "reasonable inquiry" in response to a discovery request. As Judge Gauvey explains:

> [D]efendants brought the conduct to the Court contemporaneously charging a violation of Rule 26(g), that is, that plaintiff's counsel had certified—incorrectly—in signing the response to defendants' requests for production on or about March 21, 2012, that counsel had done so "to the best of [his or her] knowledge, information and belief formed after reasonable inquiry." The Advisory Notes to Rule 26(g) provide that "the signature certifies that the lawyer has made a reasonable effort to assure that the client *has provided* all the information and documents available to him that are responsive to the discovery demand."[9]

---

[7] *Id* at *6.
[8] Peerless Indus., Inc. v. Crimson AV, LLC., No. 1:11-cv-1768, 2013 WL 85378 (N.D. Ill. Jan. 8, 2013).
[9] *Branhaven* at *2.

Plaintiff's counsel in *Branhaven* made no reasonable inquiry—they just told their client to do it. To make matters worse, in the response, the plaintiff's counsel stated that they would "make the responsive documents available for inspection and copying at a mutually convenient time."[10]

OBJECT NOW OR FOREVER HOLD YOUR PEACE

That is yet another lesson for the bar in *Branhaven*: File an objection or get an extension to a request for production. Do not just say you will produce everything as requested unless you really mean it. This is a rookie mistake, and I don't see many doing that. However, if an attorney does respond like that, then they had better deliver, which in this case they did not.

Here is Judge Gauvey's explanation of how you should respond:

> There are only three appropriate responses to a request for production of documents: (1) an objection to the scope, time, method and manner of the requested production; (2) an answer agreeing to the requested scope, time, place and manner of the production; or (3) or a response offering a good faith, reasonable alternative production which is definite in scope, time, place or manner.
>
> Plaintiff did none of the three. Rather, with its meaningless and arguably misleading response, plaintiff simply tried to buy time and technically comply with Rule 34. One of plaintiff's counsel essentially admitted as much.[11]

After many delays, the plaintiff here finally produced thousands of PDF files (flat and metadata stripped). That was equivalent to paper and could not be searched without processing. To make matters worse, there was no Bates-stamping. You know I am not a fan of Bates-stamping, which I consider an outdated relic of 19th-century technology.[12]

---

[10] *Id.*

[11] *Id.*

[12] Ralph Losey, *HASH: The New Bates Stamp*, 12 J. TECH. LAW POLICY 1 (June 2007).

However, if you produce in a paper or its equivalent, as happened here, it is needed.

The defendant in *Branhaven* had specifically asked for Tiff files that contained and load with full metadata so they could use their e-search platform. The plaintiff's excuse for not doing so was that was how the defendant produced to them. (Lame.) The plaintiff's counsel failed to mention that the defendant had first produced to plaintiff with Tiff and load (full metadata), then reproduced the same thing again in PDF at the plaintiff's request. They did that as a courtesy because the plaintiff's counsel was not going to use e-discovery review tools; they were just going to print to paper and review. Sound familiar?

SLOPPY PRACTITIONERS BEWARE

The plaintiff's failure to produce with full metadata in *Branhaven* was held to be a violation of the Rule 34(b)(2)(E)(ii) "reasonably useable form" requirement. Although the plaintiff here finally did make a production, it was late and in the wrong format. Defense counsel called it a last-minute "document dump."[13] The court agreed and concluded that plaintiff's counsel had failed to make a "reasonable effort" as required by Rule 26(g) "to assure that the client has provided all the information and documents responsive to the discovery demand." Here are Judge Gauvey's words:

> First, Branhaven delayed approximately *five* months before seeking an outside vendor from the date of the request for production. While a one month delay to allow an in house effort to access the servers might be seen as acceptable; a five month delay with its impact on the opposing party's discovery is not.
>
> Second, Branhaven is the plaintiff! Surely before initiating a lawsuit, which of course has resulted in substantial defense costs, Branhaven must have understood that it necessarily also would be subject to discovery demands with the attendant costs.

---

[13] *Id.* at *3.

> Third, Branhaven essentially misled defendants and their counsel, in its affirmative statement that responsive documents would be "available for inspection and copying at a mutually available time," while in fact not knowing what if any responsive documents there might be and when if ever they would be identified and produced.[14]

Making a document dump a couple of days before key depositions with metadata stripped was not the only "dirty trick" played by these plaintiff's counsel. They also scheduled four nonparty depositions in four different states for the same time. They did so without consultation as to defendants' counsel's availability, and with only three business days' notice. Plaintiff's counsel then cancelled all four of the depositions without explanation after, in the court's words, "defendants' counsel had scrambled to obtain, and educate, counsel for all four, within 24 hours of the depositions. Plaintiff offers no acceptable explanation of this conduct."[15] How would you react to that kind of conduct by opposing counsel?

Although Judge Gauvey did not sanction plaintiff's counsel for this deposition scheduling conduct, that was only because defendant did not make a timely objection. This kind of background behavior must have influenced Judge Gauvey's decision. It must have made it easier for her to sanction these bad boys under Rule 26(g).

Based on this record and upon motion by defense counsel for sanctions under Rule 26(g), the court held that:

> [P]laintiff's counsel in their execution of the Response to the requests for production wrongly certified that they were responding to the document requests "to the best of [their] knowledge, information and belief after reasonable inquiry. Plaintiff's counsel said he "promptly" sent the document request to his clients (ECF No. 59–3, 4 ¶ 11), but quite apparently did *no* meaningful follow-up.[16]

---

[14] *Branhaven* at *4.
[15] *Id.* at *1.
[16] *Id.* at *4.

One of the many mistakes cited in the opinion is the failure of plaintiff's counsel to ensure that their client's search included all of their e-mail systems. This seems incredible to me—and to Judge Gauvey too, who wrote:

> Plaintiff's delay in addressing the lack of access to these email servers is inexcusable. There is no more obvious and critical source of information in the 21st century than a company's email accounts. Plaintiff's counsel's failure to identify and produce this discovery in a timely fashion and in an acceptable form and manner while suggesting—if not misleading defendants—that it had identified responsive documents is sanctionable.[17]

USE OF DISPROPORTIONATE DISCOVERY AS A WEAPON

Discovery abuses are hardly new and unique to electronic discovery. Rule 26(g) was enacted to try to curb these abuses. As the Advisory Committee Note to the 1983 amendment creating Rule 26(g) pointed out:

> Excessive discovery and evasion or resistance to reasonable discovery requests pose significant problems.... The purpose of discovery is to provide a mechanism for making relevant information available to the litigants. "Mutual knowledge of all the relevant facts gathered by both parties is essential to proper litigation." *Hickman v. Taylor*, 329 U.S. 495, 507 (1947). Thus the spirit of the rules is violated when advocates attempt to use discovery tools as tactical weapons rather than to expose the facts and illuminate the issues by overuse of discovery or unnecessary use of defensive weapons or evasive responses. All of this results in excessively costly and time-consuming activities that are disproportionate to the nature of the case, the amount involved, or the issues or values at stake. Given our adversary tradition and the current discovery rules, it is not surprising that there are many opportunities, if not incentives, for attorneys to

[17] *Id.*

engage in discovery that, although authorized by the broad, permissive terms of the rules, nevertheless results in delay.

The only thing different from 1983 when these words were written and today is that now almost all documents are electronic, not paper. This rapid transformation has created even more opportunities for discovery tactics, evasion, and excessively costly and time-consuming discovery disproportionate to the case. This may be an old and underutilized rule, but it is still on the books to address the same kind of abuses in electronic form.

If you are up against an opposing counsel who, when it comes to e-discovery at least, is still playing the old game of hiding his or her head in the sand and if this conduct prejudices your client, then fight back. You do not have to prove bad faith or intent to protect your client (and the profession) by sanctioning the offenders. You only have to show they signed the discovery response in violation of the reasonable efforts requirement of Rule 26(g). There is nothing uncooperative about that.

Every discovery lawyer should read Rule 26(g) at least once a year. Here it is again in all of its once-hidden glory.

(g) Signing Disclosures and Discovery Requests, Responses, and Objections.

(1) *Signature Required; Effect of Signature.* Every disclosure under Rule 26(a)(1) or (a)(3) and every discovery request, response, or objection must be signed by at least one attorney of record in the attorney's own name—or by the party personally, if unrepresented—and must state the signer's address, e-mail address, and telephone number. By signing, an attorney or party certifies that to the best of the person's knowledge, information, and belief formed after a reasonable inquiry:

(A) with respect to a disclosure, it is complete and correct as of the time it is made; and

(B) with respect to a discovery request, response, or objection, it is:

(i) consistent with these rules and warranted by existing law or by a nonfrivolous argument for extending, modifying, or reversing existing law, or for establishing new law;

(ii) not interposed for any improper purpose, such as to harass, cause unnecessary delay, or needlessly increase the cost of litigation; and

(iii) neither unreasonable nor unduly burdensome or expensive, considering the needs of the case, prior discovery in the case, the amount in controversy, and the importance of the issues at stake in the action.

(2) *Failure to Sign.* Other parties have no duty to act on an unsigned disclosure, request, response, or objection until it is signed, and the court must strike it unless a signature is promptly supplied after the omission is called to the attorney's or party's attention.

(3) *Sanction for Improper Certification.* If a certification violates this rule without substantial justification, the court, on motion or on its own, must impose an appropriate sanction on the signer, the party on whose behalf the signer was acting, or both. The sanction may include an order to pay the reasonable expenses, including attorney's fees, caused by the violation.

CONCLUSION

Use Rule 26(g) in your practice. Follow it and point out its violations by opposing counsel. I am sure that if the clear terms are pointed out to the judge presiding over your case, then he or she will follow the rule and the holding in *Branhaven.* As more and more judges do that, it will be easier for those of us who know and live by the rules to engage opposing counsel in a cooperative endeavor.

Cooperation is the key to successful e-discovery legal practice, as the standard EDBP.com chart makes obvious by its inflated size. However, cooperation requires compliance with the rules and motions for sanctions where needed as a stick to force cooperation. A carrot alone never works in the rough-and-tumble world of litigation. Judge Grimm, who reintroduced us to old Rule 26(g) in *Mancia,* knew this very well.

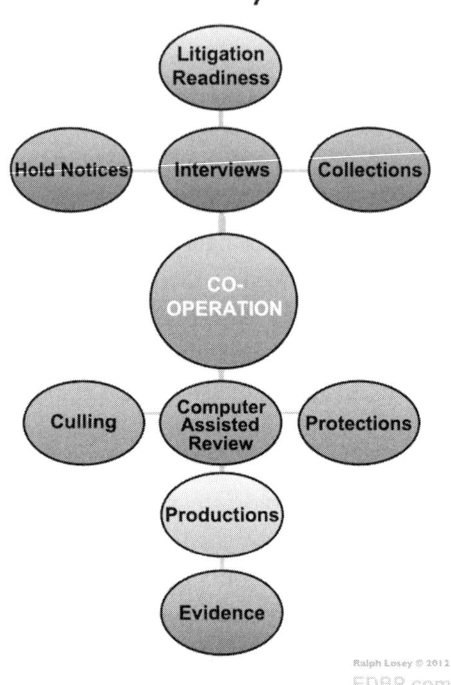

Discussion of the rule was just a side note in *Mancia* to the primary theme of cooperation. *Mancia* is one of those landmark cases in the annals of e-discovery—one that every lawyer should know by heart.[18]

Cooperation is required by the rules and the common law. Not only that, cooperation is good for your client and good for our system of justice. However, many counsel do not get it. They fight at the wrong time and with dirty tricks, like with last-minute document dumps, metadata strips, or setting and canceling depositions. For these counsel, we need routine enforcement of Rule 26(g). That is, after all, why 26(g) was enacted back in 1983. We have got to get back to that spirit and curb the discovery abuses of counsel.

---

[18]Mancia v. Mayflower Textile Services Co., 253 F.R.D. 354 (D. Md. 2008).

We should all remember Judge Gauvey's words, that "counsel has an affirmative duty to assure that their client responds completely and promptly to discovery requests." We should all pay close attention to what is happening before certifying a discovery request or discovery response.

This is a difficult challenge faced by all attorneys—both plaintiffs and defense counsel, both inside counsel and out. It is going to take a lot of conscientious work on the part of all attorneys and litigants. We need to begin by creating a clear understanding and explanation as to who is ultimately responsible for what. There is no one right answer to these questions. Each case is different. If we are doing our job right, we are in a constant state of learning, change, and adaptation. The right answer in any particular case depends on many factors and circumstances, but common to all of them is the requirement of good faith and reasonable efforts.

Index

C

D

E

F

G

H

I

J

K

L

M

N

O

P

Q

R

U

V

W

Z